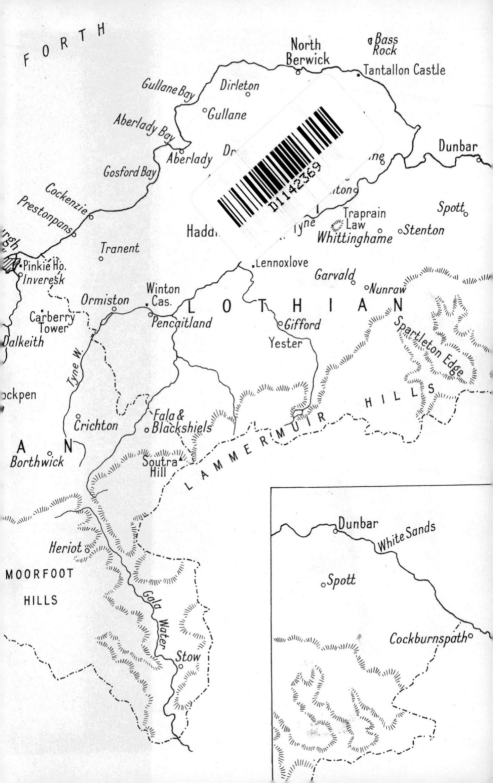

THE LOTHIANS

THE
LOTHIANS

BY

IAN FINLAY

COLLINS
ST JAMES'S PLACE, LONDON
1960

CONTENTS

ILLUSTRATIONS

7

Illustrations

CHAPTER ONE

Gateway to the Lothians

THE CLASSIC gateway to the Lothians is not the defile of Cockburnspath, where the Great North Road and the Flying Scotsman cut through the hills: it is Soutra summit. At certain seasons this can be a forbidding gateway. Nearly 1200 feet above the sea, it holds the drifted snow until the white of it grows a dirty grey like slabby limestone, and the brown water flowing from under its shrinking bulk makes runnels and moraines on the macadam of the highway. Even in summer Soutra can be forbidding. A wind hisses through the grass and darkly marbles its thousands of bleached, brown acres as squalls darken the surface of the sea. Southwards the Lammermuirs unroll an empty landscape dappled by sailing clouds or, more often, dusky under a louring grey sky. Northward, the ground tumbles towards the plain of Lothian.

At first glance, there is nothing whatever in this wilderness to mark it as the gate to anywhere: no flanking hills or obvious natural bastion, no ruinous keep or castle to confront invaders. However, if one follows a deserted sidetrack over the moor for a matter of a mile or so a little stone hut appears on a knoll by the track. It goes by the name of Soutra Aisle. Once it was part of the Holy Trinity Church and Hospital of Soutra, said to have been put there by Malcolm IV around 1164 for the use of travellers—*coenobium de Soltrey adviatores hospitandos*, as the *Scotichronicon* has it. This wealthy hospice lay across the main road out of England and the Border country into Lothian and Scotland, not to bar travellers but to rest and refresh them and send them on their way. For the old road went this way, not by the present route. Now no one comes by Soutra Aisle, its wealth has vanished, its only offerings are swatches of matted wool rubbed off on its corners by the hill-sheep sheltering in its lee from the gales, its only legible message a carved stone above the lintel

9

with the initials of one David Pringle and his wife Agnes. Pringle was a laird of these parts whose ancestor got his land from James V in return for giving him shelter and ordering his wife to kill the fattest fowl for the stranger, not knowing who he was.

Some say the view from Soutra Aisle is the finest in south Scotland. On a brisk spring morning its sweep is breath-taking, from the Isle of May in the north-east over the blue crests of the Sidlaws in the north to the dark cone of Ben Lawers and the lion-shape of Ben Ledi to the west. Below lie the fat farmlands of East Lothian, the busy waters of the Firth and the smoke-haze of the capital city.

When Agricola stood here, the burnished eagles of the Second Legion, the Adiutrix, glinting behind him in the pale northern sun, his narrowed eyes took in a great deal more than the loveliness of the view. There, beyond the blue arm of the sea, lay the country of the Picts, those Painted People who were to elude and defy Rome to the last and in the end to overrun the northern marches of her world-empire. The general's practised glance must have seen at once that Lothian is, in a sense, like a spear. If he could seize and hold it, then Rome had in her grasp a weapon with point prodding below the enemy's heart. If he failed to seize it, then the spear was reversed and became a threat to all the soft-living colonial settlements south of the Cheviots. The spear was to change hands many times in the next two thousand years. Like the plains of Lombardy or the Monastir Gap, Lothian was to become one of those fateful narrow places which ever and again drew through them the tides of great events, even altering the lives of countless men and women who never heard its name.

An hour on this summit of Soutra will make it clear why Lothian has meant what it has done to Scotland. Soutra is on the verge of that long cleavage line where the Lammermuir and the Moorfoot Hills meet the plain of the three Lothians. Southwards is the barrier of the Southern Uplands, hundreds of square miles of rolling, grassy hills. The ancient ways across this barrier were few and, with the country or the weather hostile, dangerous ; but once in Lothian an invader has direct, open passage all the way to the Carse of Stirling, in the very throat of Scotland, and with a fleet on his right flank to support and supply him if—like both Romans and English—he has command of the sea.

This corner of the Lothians is nearer to its past than is any other. Not that it is specially rich in ruins, but it seems to let the world go by it out of sight and almost out of hearing. Its parishes at their northern ends march with the prosperous and progressive farms of East Lothian, but in the south they go climbing up into the cleughs of the hills through dark, cool woods sounding with plash of stream and the pipe of birds. There are no towns on their little roads, no mill chimneys rising from their dells. These parishes are not even on the way to any-where. Their lanes twist and turn interminably, their little fields are like rumpled patchwork quilts, and their villages— some of them at least—still vie with Fife's and Dumfriesshire's as the prettiest in Scotland.

Standing sentinel between this secluded corner and the busy rest of Lothian is Traprain Law, once called Dunpender : a great reef of rock rising three or four hundred feet above the rolling fields. Sudden, isolated hills of this kind are a typical feature of the Lothian farmlands. Known to geologists as "crag-and-tails," these hills are extrusions of hard, igneous rock through softer formations which have been scoured down by the ice mass of Pleistocene times, and where they have split the slow current of the glacier they show the mark of the grinding ice of centuries as precipitous, rocky bluffs. Away to the east can be seen two famous examples of this kind of hill—Salisbury Crags and the Castle Rock of Edinburgh, towering above the grey reek of smoke that hangs over the city ; and beyond them again lie others, the Kaimes Hill and Dalmahoy. Those craggy heights were the main refuges of men in the Lothians during the thousands of years when the low ground was mainly bog and thicket. The marks of his occupation are still there—stone terrace walls so tumbled and overgrown that only an expert eye can recognise the pattern of them ; but out of the soil of them, often scratched by rabbits from their burrows, have come relics which can be used to determine the nature and succession of the waves of forgotten occupants. Traprain is the best and most complete of those monuments to a dead civilisation. It alone has produced a hoard which was a nine-days' wonder in the public Press. It alone has been the subject of a vigorous public controversy which found echoes in the House of Lords.

The subject of the controversy is an expanding road-metal quarry which, from the Haddington-Dunbar road, can be seen clearly as a scar in the flank of the hill. A protest arose against the threat of this quarry to a place which had proved to be a mine of something far more rare than road-metal. For Traprain seems to have supported a fortified township from the later Stone Age right down to Romano-British times, and out of its slopes has come a succession of pottery, bronze and silver relics now housed in the National Museum of Antiquities. Many of these are made with skill and designed with considerable artistry and spirit. They provide ample evidence that long before the Romans came here in the first century after Christ the men of Lothian were cunning craftsmen and had leisure and taste to develop their arts.

I make no apology for lingering on Traprain. It is a sort of dip-stick of prehistoric Lothian—not by any means giving samples of all that went on there before the Romans came, but at least giving us a picture of the ultimate phases. As to the dimmer past, no palæoliths have been found anywhere in the Lothians, so that in the Old Stone Age there must have been a wilderness of ice and bog; and there have been few enough flints even from Neolithic times, and no graves or sign of settlements. Only with the art of metal-working did penetration of bogs and thickets become possible and colonisation spread. Burial cairns and standing stones mark the arrival of Bronze Age man around 2000 B. C. or a little after. In the main he seems to have come across the sea from the Low Countries. His path is marked by graves where the dead are buried individually—unlike the communal burials of the west—and with his dead he buried drinking-vessels of beaker type scored or indented with patterns which can be matched in the land he came from. Those beaker folk came in all along the coast of the Firth north of Traprain. Slowly, very slowly, they penetrated inland, over a span of maybe as much as a thousand years, building their strong-points first perhaps on Traprain itself, later pressing westwards up the firth, later still building sanctuaries such as the big one on

Cairnpapple Hill near Linlithgow. Some of their works have accumulated lore and legend which cling to the stones like lichens. Near the foot of Traprain is a monolith called the Loth Stone. It is the traditional grave of King Loth, who has been given credit for the name of Lothian.

Not until 1919, however, did Traprain yield its most sensational discovery. A great square of earth had been stripped of its turf by an archæological party when the foreman of the " dig " felt his pick strike something that was neither earth nor rock. Driving it in again, he brought up on its point a metal object which, though discoloured, turned out to be a little silver bowl. Further digging disclosed a pit. In the pit lay a hoard of dirty-coloured objects embedded in what the discoverer has described as apparently a purple paste. The pit stank of sulphurous fumes. It would have been hard to guess that out of this decayed heap would emerge the richest hoard of Treasure Trove ever dug up in Scotland.

Now perhaps the most precious exhibit in the National Museum, the Traprain Treasure consists of about 160 articles of silver. Before they were buried in the pit they had been crushed and flattened into a mere dump of scrap metal, and only long and careful restoration brought them back to their original shapes. Many were too much damaged to be restored at all, others were decayed by the action of the sulphur in the soil heaped on them. But even those in a fragmentary state reveal glimpses of craftsmanship of a high order. There are flagons and bowls and dishes, platters and spoons, many of them exquisitely decorated with human and animal figures as well as with intricate patterns. Most of the scenes depicted are classical, such as episodes in the tales of Hercules ; but some are Biblical, and the chi-rho symbol of the early Christians occurs on a few of the pieces.

This lovely work was never, of course, done in the Lothians. It is Roman work, mainly of the fifth century, or just about the time of the fall of Rome. It is, in fact, loot. Some of the vessels are even torn in two : divided spoils. The shallow pit has a makeshift look and points to a hurried attempt at concealment. Certain things in the hoard seem traceable to Gaul. It may be loot from the burned-out villa of a colonial magnate. Were the pirates who brought it Saxons—those marauders against whom the Romans appointed the Counts of the Saxon Shore ? Or were they men of Lothian faring far afield in search of plunder ?

Possibly the first man to make a methodical excavation of Traprain was the great doctor who investigated the anæsthetic properties of chloroform, Sir James Young Simpson. It was not loot he dug for in 1860, however, but the grave of King Loth. In the following year a stone cist was dug up near the "Loth Stone." Loth is supposed to have been slain by the arrow of a shepherd who won the love of his daughter Thenew ; for Loth in his fury had tried to turn Traprain Law into a sort of Tarpeian Rock by having her thrown from its heights. The princess did not die but, senseless, was set adrift on the Firth where wind and tide carried her westwards to Culross. The fruit of her love for the shepherd was a son, Kentigern, who, as Mungo, travelled farther west and built the monastery around which Glasgow grew into a town. All this is supposed to have taken place early in the sixth century.

Between Traprain and the Lammermuirs lies a group of parishes which have the good fortune to be on the way to nowhere in particular. The roads twine through their dales and hollows as convolvulus twines through a hedge. They are the threshold of the Lothians, not in the physical sense of being the first part one comes to in approaching the Lothians by road or rail, but in being the least spoilt corner of the old Lothians—the only corner where life seems to move at something like the old tempo, where the whirr of reapers is commoner than the clamour of traffic and the appetising stink of middens is stronger than the lethal stench of the internal combustion engine. Here relics of the past are perhaps no more numerous than in other parts of the Lothians, but they are allowed to grow older gracefully instead of being mocked by the tawdry face of progress.

The biggest of this group of parishes is Whittinghame, which stretches from the south side of Traprain as far as the tops of the Lammermuirs and the headwaters of the Whiteadder. To most people of to-day—or yesterday ?—Whittinghame is synonymous with the name of Arthur James Balfour, whose grandfather bought the estate in 1817 and began the tale of political service which was to last more than a century. The home of the Balfours is modern. Whittinghame formerly centred on the old Tower a few hundred yards south-west of the present mansion. The Tower is the "fatal house" where in 1567 Bothwell and Maitland of Lethington came to plot the death of Darnley with the Earl of Morton, and tradition maintains the place of the plotting to be the ancient yew in the garden, despite the fact that the conspiracy was hatched at midwinter.

The sheltered cleughs and commanding heights of this parish form one of the cradles of man in the Lothians. Where its bounds embrace the Lammermuirs, most of the tops can show their cairns or their hut-circles—on Spartleton Edge, on Priestlaw Hill, Penshiel Hill, the rigs of Johnscleugh. For the unskilled eye there may be nothing to see but some tumbled boulders, but the stones speak of little communities watchful above the scarcely passable bush and swamp of the low ground which is now fat farming land. In the Middle Ages and after, folk in the snug villages by the sheltered meadows and winding streams below looked up at those heights with their crumbling remains in some awe and fear, and legends of fairies and witches seem to have flourished around here. Indeed, in the neighbouring parish of Spott the terrible witch-hunts which shadowed Scotland as they did other northern countries lingered longer than anywhere else north of the Border, and it is said the last witch executed died here. The kirk-session records for 1705—only two years before the Union, only two centuries before our own—contain the laconic entry "many witches burnt on the top of Spot Loan"; and a stone by the roadside half a mile from Spott Church marks the place where in 1698 a poor woman called Marion Lillie, the Ringwoodie Witch, was burnt "for imprecations and witchcraft." And if not witchcraft, then violence. . . . A group of ancient stones by the Priestlaw-Garvald road is called the Packman's Grave after a packman supposed to have been murdered in the inn at Danskine. But the gruesome is not confined to the lonelier parts of the parish. Shortly after the Reformation a notorious minister of Spott, John Kello by name, hung his wife one Sabbath in the manse, proceeded to the church and preached a sermon of special eloquence, the text of which is unfortunately not on record. For some time he pretended his wife had run away, but the minister of Dunbar, his suspicions aroused, one day accosted him in the words of Nathan the prophet: "Thou art the man." The Rev. Kello confessed and himself was hanged in the Grassmarket of Edinburgh.

The eerie traditions of Spott and Stenton and other places in this corner of Lothian are not hard to understand, for they lie in the shadow of the great upland mass of the Lammermuirs. Spartleton Edge, western buttress of this salient of the Southern Uplands, looks westwards to a lonely country of moors and burns scattered with cairns and stone circles which lie there like the half-buried bones of a far-off past. Circles such as the one near Zadlee and that at a thousand feet on the summit of the Edge are formed of stones which barely peep above the ground. Traditions die hard and superstition clearly clung to such places. The haunts of men retain their odours, whether of sanctity or the reverse, and one comes on ancient hill-forts like the one below Bleak Law which men of later times out of a fearful misunderstanding have dubbed the Witches' Knowe.

Hemmed between Monynut Edge and the sea lie two parishes as much cut off from the world as if they were in Caithness or Wester Ross: more, for neither the tourist nor even the tripper from Dunbar a few miles away seem to penetrate them. They are Innerwick and Oldhamstocks. Innerwick, again, has its Witches' Cairn, on the Crystal Rig, and its Witches' Knowe, scene of another burning of those poor women; but the principal feature of the parish is Innerwick Castle, now quite ruined, once defended by nine Scots gentlemen against the invading English army of Somerset. Oldhamstocks is much more interesting, in every way. It is, for a start, well tucked away in a fold of the hills, to be come at only by a steep and twisting road. The name is a queer one. It has more of an English flavour about it, and there is something English in the snug concealment of the place. The church presiding over it is not as old as some accounts would have it, but it is built on old foundations and, like many another parish church in these parts, produced at least one distinguished man—a son of the manse who under the name of Bonaventura is said to have mastered all known languages and was eventually appointed librarian in the Vatican by Pope Paul V. Below Oldhamstocks the land falls in deep, wooded denes

The Traprain Treasure—some pieces selected from the hoard of fifth-century silverwork, now preserved in the National Museum of Antiquities of Scotland

The Distance Slab from the Antonine Wall at Bridgeness

towards the sea cliffs. Near one of them is the ruined collegiate church of Dunglass, two centuries ago used as a stable yet in spite of its shattered state retaining a certain quality of hoary dignity common to so many of the little churches of the Lothians. Its foundation charter is dated 1403.

North of Lothian Edge there are deceptive folds in the ground where unexpected beauty lurks : Pressmennan Lake, for example, created in 1819 by damming a little valley in an age when the Edinburgh citizens were assiduously draining everything they could have turned into ornamental water. Biel, a little way from Pressmennan, is equally unexpected and has far more of a story behind it. This once fantastically long house—when last I saw it builders were reducing it to more manageable proportions— hides from the north winds off the Firth on the sunny slope of an east-west valley, with stands of stately timber giving it further concealment. The most significant thing in the house is a stone above the entrance on which is carved the inscription : TRADITIONIS SCO. ANNO PRIMO, 1707. Which, being inter- preted, means "In the first year of Scotland's betrayal, 1707." The stone was put there by the owner of Biel, Lord Belhaven, for in him and Fletcher of Saltoun East Lothian produced two of the fiercest and most eloquent opponents of Scotland's union with England. Belhaven's speech in the debate over the Articles of Union, with its extravagant figure of Caledonia done to death by her own friends, like Cæsar in the Senate, is less well known than Lord Marchmont's crushing retort to it—"Behold he dreamed, but when he awoke he found it was a dream! " But at the time Belhaven's speech rang through Scotland, was printed and re-printed, while even Marchmont admitted it to be a great and terrible speech. If his thoughts about the Union proved dreams, however, his dreams about Biel came true. In 1702 he brought here in a flowerpot among his baggage one of the earliest Cedars of Lebanon to find its way to Scotland. A century later it had become a stately tree. The shelter created by it and its companions formed the "micro-climate" with which many a skilled Scottish gardener made miracles possible, and the name of John Street of Biel became famous for the cultiva- tion of exotics. The blue rain of wistarias still shimmers in summer on the terraces at Biel.

In the Lammermuirs

On the west side of this buttress of the Lammermuirs the land is again rumpled into clefts and nooks where men have made themselves snug against haars and hill-mists. Garvald village is so well hid that one comes near to being justified in saying it may be stumbled upon. The burn which flows down its little valley goes by the odd name of the Papana. The derivation of this is obscure. Has it some connection with the Latin word for priest? Parts of the parish church date back to the twelfth century, and there is a Norman string-course and other fragments of the ancient building where Cistercian nuns worshipped from the reign of Malcolm IV onwards. James II granted a charter to make the nunnery into a strong place and to "have guns aye loaded to shoot at our aulden enemies of England," for Garvald is at the "home" end of the long moor road that winds across the Lammermuirs from Duns and the Border. The fortalice where the guns were mounted still exists, although restored and adapted as a mansion. This is the House of Nunraw, or Nunnerowe. It was, in its original state, for the most part built in the sixteenth century when the redoubtable Elizabeth, Prioress of Haddington, swore to resist the "auld ynemeis" or raze Nunraw to the ground. The most interesting feature of the castle came to light in 1864, when the plaster ceiling of a first-floor room was broken away during the restoration to reveal one of those rare painted ceilings which were the delight of the better Scots houses of the late sixteenth century and the early years of the seventeenth. Joists and boards are all decorated, the tempera colours being laid on a thin skin of plaster spread on the oak. In some of these ceilings the pattern is a little crude or incongruous, but at Nunraw the touch is of the lightest, the designs skilfully executed and in excellent taste. There is a row of shields with the arms of Scotland, England, France, Spain and such other states as Sicily and Denmark, to say nothing of the initials of Patrick Hepburn and his wife, Helen Cockburn, who came to Nunraw in 1595. From Nunraw south the road climbs into wilder country on Spartleton Edge, but another road winds westwards to the secluded Loch of Danskine, a mile-long tongue of water merging into a moorhen-haunted bog sometimes called Cromwell's Steps, since the Protector is supposed to have led his army across it on stepping-stones on his way to Dunbar.

Yester is perhaps the choicest parish in the Lothians. Neither railway nor main trunk road runs through it, and it sleeps in an atmosphere of the eighteenth century. In Gifford village, its chief centre, cars and buses seem anachronisms, and one feels a four-in-hand rattling up to the door of an inn would be accepted without more than a casual glance by the old men sunning themselves against white-washed walls of a summer afternoon. It is a spacious village. The mercat-cross—not a particularly notable one—still occupies the centre of the square ; and the village has the air, rare enough in Scotland, of living on the fringe of a courtly manor conducted in the style of a more gracious age. Indeed the feu-charters of some of the houses in the village may still, for all I know, contain those clauses which, until recently at least, required the tenants to work for a day winning the hay in the parks of Yester and even to attend the Marquess for two days yearly " sufficiently mounted with horse and arms," an exemplary clause in these unstable times of rocketing rates and crazy cost-of-living indices. The Marquess here is the Marquess of Tweeddale. The manor is Yester House, a fine eighteenth-century building in the midst of a park, brought into relationship with the village by means of the shady avenue of trees, the scheme being completed by a handsome church built in 1710. There was an older church, and an older village, on the site, indeed the older books claim it as the birthplace of John Knox himself, perhaps mainly on the strength of his friend Beza's reference to him as " Giffordiensis." The most notable man of the Church born in the village for certain, however, is John Witherspoon. After a distinguished ministry in Scotland, Witherspoon was invited to become President of the College of New Jersey, now the University of Princeton, where he put the training course for the clergy in the United States on a new basis, a more solid and a sounder basis, from the discipline of which emerged some of America's greatest men. In 1776 Witherspoon went as representative of New Jersey to Congress, and helped to draft the Declaration of Independence. The *Statistical Account* reminds us that this parish also produced another distinguished American divine, Dr. Charles Nisbet, President of the College of Carlisle ; but his transplantation seems to have been less successful than Dr. Witherspoon's, since the *Account* adds that he wrote to his friends at home that America was certainly a land of promise, for it was "all promise and no performance."

The gates to Yester are a fine pair, simple and monumental, in the manner of Robert Adam, perhaps actually to his design, and the house itself is an early classical essay on the model of Kinross House in Fife, although very different from it. It belongs, says a recent writer, "to that distinguished group of houses, including Inverary and Penicuik, which celebrate the advanced and liberal ideas which brought about the Union." This odd assertion seems to arise from the fact that Yester was built for the second Marquess, a strong Union man. As we have just seen, Lord Belhaven, at Biel a few miles away, was quite as advanced and liberal in his notions of improvement, but opposed the Union tooth and nail! Yester, however, went on building until the year when the French Revolution broke out. The slaters on the roof are said to have thrown their slates at the fugitives chased from the field of Prestonpans by the Highlanders in 1745, and both William Adam and Robert himself were to leave their marks on the house. Between them, father and son designed the splendid decorations of the interior, and the saloon, with its Palladian ceiling and golden walls, combines magnificence with the subtle colour-tones of Culzean. The Tweeddale family has owned the lands of Yester for six centuries. They obtained them by marriage with the Giffords. Ruined Yester Castle is fabled as the work of a wizard, Sir Hugo Gifford, celebrated by Scott in *Marmion.* Small wonder it caught Scott's fancy, for the ruin rises from a tongue or rock between the Hopes Water and a converging tributary stream, with gloomy woods shrouding the valley sides around. The portion principally associated with Sir Hugo and his black arts is reached by a worn stone stair leading steeply downwards . . .

> Of lofty roof and ample size,
> Beneath the castle deep it lies :
> To hew the living rock profound,
> The floor to pave, the arch to round,
> There never toil'd a mortal arm,
> It all was wrought by word and charm ;

And I have heard my grandsire say,
That the wild clamour and affray
Of these dread artisans of hell
Whose labours under Hugo's spell
Sounded as loud as ocean's war
Among the caverns of Dunbar.

This extraordinary chamber in the rock is the famed Goblin Ha',
or the Bo-Hall, as Fordoun refers to it. This strange rib-vaulted
hall was referred to by the late Professor Hannah as perhaps one
of the most important buildings in the history of Scottish
architecture, a thirteenth-century structure anticipating the
manner of the late fourteenth century.

Before Gifford village came into being in the seventeenth
century the site was occupied by the medieval township of
Bothans, which lent its name to the parish too. All that survives
is the old kirk, east of Yester mansion. Yester woods shelter it,
and the Gifford Water runs close by. A few fragments of an
older church are built into it—two beasts in the east gable, for
example—and the original church seems to have been consecrated
in 1241. For six hundred years at least it has been linked with the
name of the Hay family, and it is still the mortuary chapel of
the Tweeddales. The last parish service was held there in 1710,
for in that year the new parish kirk of Gifford was completed
by the Marquess of Tweeddale, when some of the furniture of
the old kirk was transferred to the new : perhaps the old bell of
1492, certainly the old pulpit with its sounding-board, although
the local tradition that Knox preached in it is even less likely
than that the Reformer was a Gifford man, for pulpits of this
style belong to the seventeenth century.

If Soutra is the gate of Lothian, then Lammer Law is the
gatepost. It is no dramatic peak by Highland standards, splitting
the skyline, but its 1700-odd feet top its neighbours and indeed
all other crests of the Lammermuirs, and it is a wild enough
piece of sheeprun to be within sight of the spires of Edinburgh.
Out of its flanks come the Hopes Water and many another burn
that refreshes the fat fields of the East Lothian plain, and it is
one of the small company of high places which can give a climber
a draught of chill spring water miraculously near its top.

On Soutra itself the burghers and farmers of the plains have kept a weather eye for many a century. They say the stooks in the fields about Haddington were set end-on towards it to take less harm from the storms of wind and rain that Soutra sent down at harvest time, but invading armies too have come by this road since early times, while many a man doomed to a lost cause has climbed it going southwards, from the Flodden host to Charles Edward's Highlandmen, who are said to have eaten and drunk at the inn called Lourie's Den. Soutra, of course, is in a sense more deserted now than ever since the Middle Ages. The cars and long-distance transport of the mid-twentieth century whine up or down its gradient taking nothing from its windy spaces but the oxygen, giving nothing back but acrid fumes which mercifully disperse in a trice. In the first decade of Victoria's reign, when the highway was new, thirteen stagecoaches rolled up and down the hill every day. Twenty pairs of horses were stabled at the Blackshiels Inn, to say nothing of a spare coach or two and gigs and traps ; while farmers from Lauderdale stopped there on their way back from the Thursday Dalkeith market to drink their gains or drown their losses until their wives came by on their way to church on the Sunday and dragged them out to straighten them up for the sermon. There have been times, too, when men kept an eye on Soutra for reasons other than the weather.

> Those on Soutra Edge shall see the fire of
> Eggerhope Castle, and make taiking in like
> manner, and then may all Lothian be warned.

Thus an Act of Parliament of 1455, commanding the lighting of one faggot for the approach of an English army, two faggots if the army be coming indeed, and four in a row if they come in great force. The Armada, too, brought warning fires on Soutra ; so did the threatened invasion by Napoleon.

West of Soutra lies the Moor of Fala, a bleak, rolling tableland rising to a thousand feet and centred on a lochan called Fala Flow, a black, peaty stretch of water to which the wild duck come in numbers. The moor seems to have been the scene of the first of those final episodes which broke James V's heart and brought his early death. Here he camped with his army on his way to do battle with Henry VIII, and here he urged unity on his barons in the face of danger; but the barons would not listen, and James had to return from Fala a disheartened man. Fala indeed, or this lonely part of it, seems always to have disheartened men, for there are almost no signs of early habitation on it except the fragment of a building known as Fala Luggie, or Lodging. The Luggie has been confidently called Roman, even in print, on the strength of a couple of Roman urns found in the vicinity a century ago, but it is probably no older than the seventeenth century.

West of Fala Moor, again, comes the next great route into Lothian, the Lauder road. Here the county of Midlothian makes a salient southwards, deep into the Southern Uplands, taking in a slice of country which seems to belong with the Borders and is out of reach of that sharp, salt smell of the sea which at times pervades the rest of the Lothians. Here alone is a river draining out of Lothian, taking virtue from its acres to feed the meadows of Tweeddale and the salmon of the Tweed. Somewhere in the upland farmlands of Nettingflat the Gala Water has its beginnings and flows off down the long, increasingly fertile vale between Lammermuirs and Moorfoots which in days long past was called the Stow of Wedale. There is some dispute about the origin of the name Wedale, but I for one am quite ready to accept the simple derivation given by the Rev. David Weddell in the *Statistical Account* of 1845. He connects it with the Anglo-Saxon *wae*, for woe or sorrow, with the suffix dale. Probably this main route between south and north saw many a " sanguinary affray," as he delicately puts it. From Heriot, river, road and railway wind down the vale in long, gentle curves to the steepled village of Stow itself. Legend associates Wedale with King Arthur, and Nennius states that fragments of the true cross brought from the Holy Land by the king were deposited in the Church of the Virgin Mary of Wedale, a church the ruins ·of which—or a fragment of them—are sometimes claimed to lie near the mansion of Torsonce, half a mile south of Stow; but the main relic left behind by Celts in Wedale is the broch at Bow Castle, about a mile below Torsonce. H. M. Chadwick points to this and the one or two other examples of the broch in south-east Scotland as evidence of an invasion of the northern

Picts—clearly the spear of Lothian, dropped by the enfeebled hand of Rome, was turned about and thrust down the ways by which the Romans had come. The Bow Castle broch stands high above the Gala Water, or once stood so, for now there is little more than a segment of dry-stone wall and a scattering of stones probably used as a ready-made quarry over a thousand years. One fragment of typical broch pottery and some sherds of Roman vessels found on the site help to fill in a little one's vision of this fort as a Pictish outpost on the fringes of the Imperial dominion, but the most appealing relic dug up is a little enamelled cock-brooch belonging to that most masterly era in northern art, the Late-Celtic. It can now be seen in the National Museum of Antiquities.

On both sides of Wedale the high hill pastures have been reckoned rich and profitable ever since the Middle Ages. There was many a wild fight between the herds of this manor and that over the rights of pannage and pasturage on those hills, culminating in a scandalous feud between the monks of Melrose—richest of all the Scottish foundations, and at one time boasting more sheep than any English house except the rival Cistercian one of Fountains—and the men of Wedale. William the Lion brought it to an end in 1184, when he imposed the Peace of Wedale, although the doughty friars of the abbey were soon at it again, to the extent of invading Wedale and slaughtering a priest there. To the west of Wedale the hills are far more extensive and fill most of the twin parishes of Stow and Heriot. They are fine hills. The southern boundary of Lothian runs along heights the tops of which twice break the two-thousand-foot level, heights with fine, wild names to them such as Windlestraw Law and Blackhope Scar. This is perhaps the loneliest, least-known corner of the Lothians, the only road through it the twisting one from Heriot to Innerleithen, which climbs to a summit of more than 1200 feet near Eastside Heights, a mere dozen miles or so as the crow flies from the traffic of Edinburgh streets. To get among these hills direct from Wedale, one must follow the Luggate Water from where it joins the Gala, almost opposite Torsonce. Clearly the name means the "low gate," in Scots the low road, and in ancient times this pleasant glen seems to have been fairly populous, for all the way there are remains of enclosures and hut-circles, if the only medieval structure was Ewes Castle, now reduced to some scattered stones.

The Luggate rises not far from the summit of the Innerleithen road. This is the heart of the Moorfoots, on the other side of whose watershed is one of the Capital's great catchment areas. Edinburgh is peculiarly well placed for her water supply, with an average rainfall as low as London's—about 25 inches —yet possessing a catchment area only a few miles away with a rainfall approaching twice that figure. In the shadow of Torfichen Hill and Maudslie lies the great island-studded reservoir of Gladhouse, with smaller lochs at Rosebery and Edgelaw, a mile or two nearer Edinburgh. Gladhouse might well be a Highland loch, and there are good trout in it too. Like the parish of Heriot, the parish of Temple in its southern parts is very much a border march of Lothian, and this hilly country is largely given over to the sheep and the whaups, with hardly even a scattered ruin, save only Hirendean Castle, a thousand feet up on a shoulder of Blackhope Scar.

The northern end of Temple parish makes a very different picture. The road coming down from Gladhouse wanders through a rolling, windswept country, a country of upland farms and stane dykes such as William Gillies, who lives in the midst of it, has translated into those lyrical, sensitive water-colours which have made him one of the first painters in Scotland. Down the road dips among stands of ancient trees, first at Rosebery, then in the woods about Temple village itself. In a few moments the South Esk has ceased to be a hill-burn and become a little brown river at the bottom of a wooded gorge. Buried deep in this gorge are the ruins of a pretty fourteenth-century church of pale, warm stone with here and there some finely-carved mouldings. The name of the village derives from the fact that the land once belonged to the Knights Templars of Jerusalem. This order was suppressed in 1312, and the Knights of St. John took over, but the little church in the valley must be the only surviving relic of the Templar foundation left in Scotland.

East of Temple lies one of the innermost and strongest gateways to the heart of the Lothians, from the Middle Ages at least. It lies across the Galashiels road, the road from Wedale, where this comes down from Heriot and the hills to fork left and right down the valleys of the Gore and the Tyne. It is, therefore, not one gateway but twin gateways, each defended by a powerful fortress.

The first and the more impressive of the two fortresses is Borthwick Castle. It juts from a knoll once called the Mote of Lochorwart or Lochwarret, and in failing light it looks more like some natural outcrop of the living rock than a structure of man's devising. Indeed, it is probably the best-built castle in Scotland, with the stones beautifully graded from base to top and walls twelve feet thick, the fine packing of them exposed on the east side by Cromwell's cannon in 1650. The twin towers stand well over a hundred feet to the crests of their stone-slabbed roofs. Only a few narrow windows break the vast faces of the masonry, over which loom the shadows of the corbelled cornices which carry the parapet walk where sentinels could watch for signal fires on the battlements of the second guardian fortress to be described presently—Crichton, a couple of miles away. It was in 1430 that Sir William of Borthwick received a licence from James I to build on the Mote "a castle or fortalice, to surround it with walls and ditches, to defend it with gates of brass and iron." Sir William, later Lord Borthwick, had an honoured career, though a less dramatic one than his neighbour, Chancellor Crichton; and, if we are to accept the *Statistical Account*, the fine effigies of a knight and his lady in Borthwick church are those of Lord and Lady Borthwick—effigies remarkable not only for their carving but for the traces of gold and colours which made the monument magnificent five centuries ago.

The castle's most romantic hour came shortly after the Reformation. The Baron Borthwick of the time was as obstinately opposed to the new faith as the stones of his castle were to invaders of the Lothians. Not that he did not share the popular scorn against a corrupt priesthood, for in 1547 that magnificent hall of the castle seems to have seen the enactment of that odd practice known as the Feast of the Tipsy Priest. Carved on the Montrose Panels in the National Museum of Antiquities are some queer little figures of cloaked foxes or swine thought to be satiric representations of priests; but I have small doubt they depict some such strange rite as took place at Borthwick, when

servants garbed as beasts brayed and roared and played fiddles
and bagpipes around a caricature of a priest dubbed the Abbot
of Unreason. On this occasion an emissary of the See of St.
Andrews had brought letters of excommunication against Lord
Borthwick himself, but the Abbot of Unreason had him ducked
in the Gore Burn and forced him to eat the excommunicatory
parchment, first softened in a bowl of wine, assuring him that
any further letters of the same sort would " a' gang the same
gait." Twenty years later, however, his son, the sixth baron,
risked the anger of the Protestant Lords when he gave shelter at
Borthwick to Queen Mary and Bothwell, fleeing from Holyrood-
house with Morton and the others at their heels. The pursuers
surrounded the castle in the night, but Bothwell had already
escaped to Dunbar. Morton did not attempt to take the Queen,
and afterwards gave this as proof that he had no designs upon
her ; but the next day she escaped disguised as a youth, was met
by Bothwell at Cakemuir Castle below the Moor of Fala, and
began the journey that was to end in Lochleven Castle. Even
so, she was almost rescued, and among the armed band of
horsemen who thundered down to the water's edge only in
time to see the doors of the island fortress close behind their
mistress was Lord Borthwick.

Borthwick Castle is still lived in. Its hall's high, pointed roof,
with deep-embrasured windows and huge, canopied fireplace
rising from squat columns may not appeal to modern notions of
comfort, but like many another ancient house it has more in its
favour, domestically-speaking, than meets the eye. But the
oddest chapter in its history is the least known. During World
War II it became the repository of the bulk of Scotland's art
treasures. Hundreds upon hundreds of numbered crates were
stacked in its chambers—crates filled with priceless porcelain
and sculpture, superb metalwork, rich lacquers and jades from
the East, furniture from Machiavelli's Italy and the France of
the Grande Monarque, tapestries more precious than any the
Lords of Borthwick hung on these walls, to say nothing of
thousands of irreplaceable books and manuscripts. And instead
of the sentinels on the battlements were squads of watchmen,
dividing their attention between listening by night for the
throb of possible raiders in the skies and seeing to it by day that

temperature and humidity or the insidious touch of damp should not harm the treasures in their keeping.

Crichton Castle, the second fortress of this gateway to the Lothians, juts from a hillside above the headwaters of the Tyne. Unlike Borthwick, it is ruinous. It had been roofless and crumbling for long years before Sir Walter Scott trod its courts and halls and wrote of it in his great poem as " a lodging fit for Marmion's rank." The tower, oldest part of the castle, seems to be the work of the greatest of all the Crichtons : Sir William, Chancellor to the Poet King, James I, and his son. An able and cunning diplomat at a time when most men relied on their swords to win them prowess, he journeyed to Norway and France in his masters' service and won himself a peerage for his work. He had few scruples. In the great hall of the castle, with its fireplace resembling Borthwick's, he gave lavish entertainment to the two young Douglases who were to be the victims of the notorious Black Dinner in Edinburgh Castle, when Crichton saw to it that his king's most powerful rival house was dealt a treacherous blow. His grandson, the third Lord Crichton, inherited the love of intrigue. His wife was a great beauty, and there is a tangled tale of her seduction by James III, to which Crichton retorted by seducing the king's favourite sister, Princess Margaret, and by twice turning traitor. Outlawed, he fled and suffered confiscation of his estates. So the castle passed from the possession of the Crichtons for ever.

Inside, the castle holds a surprise. In contrast to the windy Lothian hillside, the interior courtyard transports one instantly to some Italian piazza, for the north wall is colonnaded with round arches, the stones above being deep cut in facets which, under slanting sun, turn this building into something unlike any other in the north. Hannah has to go to the church of Gesu Nuovo in Naples for a parallel, although the Rathaus at Lübeck has been cited as another. But Italy is the source of the exotic essay. In 1581 Francis Stewart returned from Italy to be created by James VI Earl of Bothwell and Admiral of Scotland. Initials cut above the two central pillars of the colonnade represent Francis and his wife, Margaret Douglas, while anchors point to his office of admiral.

Between them, Borthwick and Crichton, flanking the way

into the heart of the Lothians, offer the ingenious-minded a nice pair of symbols. The tenants of the one, loyal supporters of the sovereign throughout, have continued in their tenancy and their house remains intact, but for the honourable scar made by Cromwell's guns. The other, raised and dwelt in by a succession of intriguers, has changed hands repeatedly and, neglected, has crumbled into noble ruin.

CHAPTER TWO

Red Soil and Grey

THE FARMLANDS of East Lothian are among the most fertile in the world. They have bred stout men as well as heavy-cropping grains and greens, but all the stirring events and characters that go to making their history seem deep-planted in their rich, well-husbanded soils.

"Such cornfields and fields of turnips, such turnips in those fields, such stackyards!" exclaimed Cobbett in his admiration at the East Lothian farms. It was not always so. The thought and sweat of more than a hundred years had gone into the making of such results. There were big areas of bog to be drained, as many a farm with muir in its name signifies, some of the soils are cold and heavy, and the climate is by no means as encouraging as the rainfall statistics seem to suggest. Like some other narrow places, Lothian is an exposed draughty spot where crops and beasts and men must be lusty to survive. Many are the days from April to September when from Soutra or the brow of Traprain Law one can see nothing in all the plain below for the chill, white shroud of the haar, that sea mist which comes up the Firth as though it were a giant funnel drawing the salt spume from the surface of the entire North Sea. There are people who like the haar. Indeed, the salt tang of it might almost be called the scent of spring in these parts. But only those who live in the Lothians know the blight it casts, blotting out the sun or making a pale, wan platter of it, without power to warm earth or being, driving those who can into going the few miles across the hills to Peebles, where like as not they will bask under a blue sky. I well remember suggesting to the late Sir Frank Mears that the first proposal in his South-East Scotland Plan should be a towering draught-screen between Inchkeith and the Bass to keep off the haar . . . But this corridor of the Lothians is open at both ends. The prevailing west winds in their turn come soughing through from the west coast, for the Lothians are the only portion of eastern Scotland which have no mountain-masses to shield them from storms and rains generated over the Atlantic.

The rich lands stretch from Dunbar in the east to Drem and beyond to the west : a tiny " farm-belt," but so intensively worked that it is known to agriculturalists across the world. In city greengrocers in summer few " earlies " can match those smooth, well-bred-looking potatoes with a dusting of the red soil of Dunbar still clinging to them. They bring £1 per ton more than the same potatoes from other places. In spring the new-turned fields hereabout proclaim their richness, lying like pink or plum-coloured corduroy over hills and dales. Dykes, houses and whole villages are of the same red sandstone that has gone to make the fields, so that the green budding hedgerows and the blue sky and the very twinkle of the gulls wheeling and screaming in the wake of the ploughs take on value and meaning which are not in them in drabber spots. The Dunbar red land is, says T. Bedford Franklin, " the only soil in which complete perfection in potato growing could be attained," and the acreage under roots and potatoes in East Lothian is, for example, something like four times as much as the root and potato acreage in Leicestershire.

It was in the grey soils farther west, however, that so much farming history was made. Here Scotland first responded to the taunt of being a poor partner in the Union of 1707 by sowing seeds of her agricultural revolution. Under the aisle in the parish church of Saltoun is the vault of the Fletcher family, who first came to the village in the seventeenth century in the person of that doughty judge, Lord Innerpeffer, and in the vault lies the great Andrew Fletcher, who died in 1716. As a youth he had the fortune to sit at the feet of another great man, Gilbert Burnet, the young Episcopal minister of Saltoun. Burnet was destined to become Professor of Divinity in Glasgow at the age of 27, to go as a preacher to London, where he wrote the great *History of the Reformation* that brought him into collision with Pope and Swift, chided Charles II for his immorality, and was finally created Bishop of Salisbury by William of Orange. The keen mind and questing liberalism of Dr. Burnet assuredly fired Andrew

Fletcher. Like the doctor, he opposed Charles and Lauderdale. He sided with Monmouth and spent years in exile, in Holland, in Spain, even in Hungary fighting the Turks, and his sword seems to have been as sharp and as ready as his intellect. He came back with Dutch William in 1688; but he was a limited-monarchy man and even a republican, and a furious opponent of the Union of 1707 from conviction that it could only result in the domination of Scotland by England as the Union of 1603 had done. His wisdom and eloquence, paired with Lord Belhaven's, failed. A revulsion against public life set in, but as a result he applied his great mind to the family estates at Saltoun. In 1710 he sent James Meikle to Holland to acquire the art of milling barley, and the result was those winnowing fans which local ministers cried out against, calling them the Devil's wind. Opposed by old prejudices though they might be, those contrivances and all the others which followed them—more than one invented by the Meikles—helped to pull the country out of the black despair of the famine years which, because of a succession of dreadful seasons, preceded and helped to precipitate the Union. Incidentally, Saltoun Mill, where pot barley was first prepared in Scotland, still stands with its great timber wheel. Towards the end of the eighteenth century James Meikle's son, Andrew, completed his experiments with a threshing-machine. Worked by water-power or by a team of horses, it threshed from twenty to forty bushels an hour. Costly as it was—£80 was the price—it worked out cheaper than hand labour on large farms. In a few years there were 350 of Meikle's machines on the big East Lothian farms, and soon they were in use wherever there were corn crops in Scotland.

The condition of Scottish agriculture before Fletcher's time was pitiful. Even in East Lothian the high ground was nothing better than rough moorland, and the meadows were marshland off which, in dry seasons, a little hay might be taken; while the ground around the villages was held by the run-rig system—long strips of ground which gave a succession of bere, oats and pease crops, rested one year in four by letting the weeds go wild. But, as Defoe saw on his travels, the real trouble was the tenure system. The crofters could be turned off their land at any time, had no inducement to improve it even if they had had the money and

The Mercat Cross and fine eighteenth-century church at Gifford

The Italianate courtyard of Crichton Castle

knowledge ; and the landlords—the smaller ones at least—themselves had no capital, for they had their rents in kind. It bred indifference and laziness. John Cockburn of Ormistoun's comment on one such small farmer is on record : "His Husbandry goes no further than to gett bad grain one year and worse the next." Cockburn's father, Adam, Lord Justice-Clerk under Queen Anne, shrewdly saw the root of the trouble and granted long leases to two of his tenants during the famine years. One of them, Robert Wight, responded and passed on his zeal for improvement to his son, just as the the Lord Justice-Clerk did to John Cockburn.

Cockburn of Ormistoun transformed the face of his parish. In striving to get rid of the bad old infield and outfield system, in which the nearer fields got such manure as came from byre and stable and the further ones were unfed, he co-operated with Alexander Wight in enclosing the fields by hedges of earth and quicksets, filling them with thorn and bramble, rose and honeysuckle, and planting ash-trees at intervals, with a wisdom part-learned and part-instinctive which, in these days of wire fences, has been lost. Some of the timber still standing in the parish may have been of his planting, too. In a letter to his gardener dated 30th September, 1742, he writes : "I told you where I would have Elms, and where I would have chiefly Oaks, with one Ash to two Oaks and one Beech to four Ashes. You may put one Oak among the Elms to ten of the Elms and about 6 Beeches dropp'd among the Elms." Those letters to his gardener have become classics of their kind, minute in instruction, trenchant in criticism. On the model of the Honourable Society of Improvers in the Knowledge of Agriculture in Scotland, Cockburn in 1736 founded the Ormistoun Society, which met in the village inn to discuss farming topics and pool knowledge. Among its members were the eccentric judge, Lord Monboddo, and Colonel Gardiner, prominent nine years later at the Battle of Prestonpans. There was a stirring among the landlords of the county which, over the span of the century, turned poverty into riches.

The Cockburns have gone from Ormistoun : John was the last of them to live there ; but Ormistoun is the creation of the Cockburns. To walk up the wide village street under the tall trees which line it is to feel again the personality which flows out of the plain, practical and yet somehow elegant language of the letters to the gardener, for Cockburn built, or had much to do with the building of, the Town of Orm, as he called it. "Write to me particularly who is going on with Building, and how they advance," he demands. "Let me also know when G. Ramsay opens his house, and how he goes on in it and in Brewing, and if his house is in order and his Customers pleased." The village cross is not of his time, but of the fifteenth century. The old church of St. Giles was overrun by the Ormistoun Hall orchards in the seventeenth century and nothing remains but a fragment, including an arched window of the thirteenth century and, in a recess, a really fine monumental brass—a very rare thing in Scotland—exquisitely inscribed in a style that reminds one of the much more celebrated memorial to the Regent Moray in St. Giles' Kirk in Edinburgh. The lengthy Latin epitaph was composed by George Buchanan. The subject of it is Alexander Cockburn, who died young just a year or two after the Reformation. He was a pupil of Knox himself, and not Knox only but Wishart preached in this little church. Wishart, indeed, was asleep in the older House of Ormistoun when he was taken by the order of Cardinal Beaton, shortly after to be burned at St. Andrews.

To-day, the East Lothian plain is mainly devoted to arable, and the farms are fairly large ones : from 250 to 500 acres and upwards. Near the coast the lighter soils are given to early potatoes, and the farmer keeps many fattening cattle so as to get the great quantities of manure needed to give the potato fields not less than 15 tons to the acre. Numbers of these farms grow potatoes in the same fields year after year—in one case a half-century of continuous cropping has been passed—and the period between June or July and the autumn is used for a rye-grass catchcrop, dug in as green manure ; but eelworm has forced some farmers to rotate their crops. Soils are naturally fertile and usually deep, the scourings of the great glaciers which once upon a time crept eastwards through the Forth basin. Consequently, harvests are heavy. 30 cwt. and even 40 cwt. per acre are taken with grain crops. Sugar-beet, which has been grown much more since the war, yields 12 tons and even a higher return :

indeed beet has to some extent driven out turnips and swedes, which have proved subject to disease. Barley is the principal cereal, accounting for a third of the ploughed acreage, which is not surprising since brewing has one of its greatest centres in Edinburgh, a dozen miles away. The nearness of Edinburgh has also fostered a good deal of fine dairy farming, such as at Fenton Barns, near Drem, the bedding-straw problem being simplified by the widespread arable farming. The name of Fenton Barns, incidentally, is associated with one of the greatest of all Lothian farmers, George Hope. Hope's grandfather leased Fenton Barns in 1796. For twenty years the land was cleared and limed and the cold, clarty clay assiduously drained. George himself took over the farm about 1830, his father being an invalid ; but such a model did he make it that for a generation pupils came to it from England and the Continent to learn the secrets of East Lothian's agricultural reputation—its famous six-crop rotation : corn, potatoes, turnips and swedes, clover and rye-grass, and a heavy stock of winter beasts which made it possible to dress the fields with 40 tons of farmyard manure to the acre. The end came in 1865, when Hope agreed to oppose Lord Elcho in the parliamentary election. His platform, naturally, was an agricultural one, and included better conditions for the workers and security for the tenant. But he sacrificed his own security. Elcho won the election but, offended by the strength of his opponent's challenge, he induced Hope's landlord to end an exemplary tenancy of three generations, to the anger of all Scotland.

The agrarian revolution and the richness, whether red or grey, of the East Lothian fields to-day, is apt to make one forget that these lands were well husbanded in the Middle Ages too, though between the two periods they went back in part to bog and briar. The monks of Haddington and of the Border abbeys brought much of East Lothian under cultivation. In the Middle Ages only monkish farmers could devote themselves consistently to their task, for even when there was no war an incident such as Alan of Winton's seizure of the Seton heiress took a hundred pairs of hands from the plough in Lothian for a considerable time. Mention of Winton, indeed calls attention to some of the fine old houses of this part of the Lothians, which themselves suggest a certain amount of long-standing rural wealth.

Winton House itself, in Pencaitland parish, is one of Scotland's outstanding pieces of Renaissance architecture. Its tall, twisted chimneys and classic touches, seen from across the River Tyne, give it momentarily an English look, but the lack of great transomed windows, the crow-stepped gables and the tower bring one back to Scottish earth, and then come memories of Heriot's Hospital in Edinburgh, creation of the same architect, William Wallace, who died in 1631, before his two memorable works were completed. Winton was the jointure house of the Setons until they were attainted in the rising of the ' Fifteen. Externally, the architectural details are very like those of Heriot's. The house has two magnificent rooms in the best style of the period, the drawing-room and King Charles's Room. Both have fine carved stone fireplaces, and the plaster work of the ceilings is evidently from the moulds responsible for the ceilings at Pinkie House in Musselburgh and Moray House, Edinburgh. Charles I is said to have slept at Winton on his visit to Scotland in 1633.

A less imposing but in some ways more interesting mansion in the same parish is Penkaet Castle, better known as Fountainhall. This is buried behind acres of trees, and the road to it is rather a roundabout one, but there is no better example in the county of a rambling Scottish country house of the early years of the seventeenth century, turreted and dormered and crow-stepped, sun and shadow sharply contrasted in corbel and recess. There is no grandeur about it—the main entrance door would force any but an undersized man to stoop—but the house is full of character and charm and—I write in 1956—could be made enchanting, both in itself and in its setting. The builder of the original part of the house, the west wing, was Robert Pringle of Woodhead. He had these lands from the King in 1638, a date which is carved in two places on the stone, but the west wing looks to be a generation or more older. Before the end of the century the house passed into the hands of John Lauder of Fountainhall, an Edinburgh merchant, whose advocate son became Sir John Lauder and later sat on the bench as Lord Fountainhall. Fountainhall is one of that group of East Lothian worthies whose names link the rich soil of their lands with the inner councils of the nation and tempt one to believe that heavilydunged acres produce rich crops of higher commodities than barley and potatoes. Fountainhall's writings were voluminous, ranging from his gossipy and quaintly-spelt journals to collections of legal decisions. He built on the east wing and sat in a great apartment there, 43 feet long. When I saw it, it had become a mere store-room, with rare panelling stacked here and there against the walls to collect cobwebs ; but it is not hard to see the great man sitting there with his cronies of a Saturday night, having ridden down from Edinburgh through gathering winter dusk, his large mouth wet with mulled claret while he discoursed in the rambling manner of the journals of the French methods of frying eggs, leading naturally to the tale of " Christophorus Colomba " and the New World. The other rooms in the house are mostly small, the stone stairs narrow and spiral. There is, I am told, even a ghost which has been known to disarrange the bed-clothes in an upper room night after night, although the door was secured. Several of the doors are notable, incidentally, for retaining their original iron snecks.

The assumption that Pencaitland was a comfortable parish is reflected in a village kirk which shows modest but steady accretions from the thirteenth century onwards, and it is still in use. Part of the tower may even be twelfth century. There is a small thirteenth-century aisle. There are fourteenth, fifteenth and sixteenth-century buttresses, and many seventeenth-century features, including an oak pulpit, panelling and pew backs, to say nothing of a bell inscribed : *Pencaitland feare ye the Lord* 1638. In its beginning, the church belonged to the convent of Kelso.

At the eastern limit of the rich lands of East Lothian is one of the most graciously beautiful parishes in the county : White-kirk and Tyninghame. Its natural beauty is still largely a monument to one of the greatest of the improvers, Thomas, sixth Earl of Haddington, and perhaps even more to his countess, a sister of the first Earl of Hopetoun. Before their time, much of the exposed land north of Belhaven Bay was little more than a rabbit warren—sandy fields riddled with burrows and exposed to the salty blasts of the north-east gales. This was called the Muir of Tyninghame. It was Lady Haddington's persistence which at last got the Earl to enclose this ground in 1707, planting it with trees which were developed from three centres. This plantation grew into the famous Binning Woods, now unhappily cut down, and Lord Haddington resolved no longer "to fight with bad land," but planted with trees everything which he could not cultivate. He must have had the arboricultural equivalent of green fingers, for he tells how he could make his favourite oaks thrive anywhere—"on rich, poor, middling, heathy, gravelly, clayey, mossy, spouty and rocky ground, nay, even upon dry sand." Walter Scott, who often stayed with his friend the eighth earl, another Thomas, who built the present Tyninghame House, a red sandstone, neo-gothic structure, evidently made the tree-planting earl his model for the Laird of Dumbiedykes, putting into his mouth the now-celebrated advice to his son : "Jock, when ye hae naething else to do, ye may be sticking in a tree, it will be growing when ye are sleeping." What with Tyninghame and Newbyth estates, there were at the time of the second *Statistical Account* something like a thousand acres of fine timber in the parish, forming a vast windbreak against haar and storm, and further all-seasons protections were given by the holly hedges which were to become so noted —nearly three thousand yards of them—judiciously set on welldrained ground in a light loam. But the stately woods and parks of this east neuk of Lothian are linked with a tradition of excellent agriculture which reached a climax in the middle of the nineteenth century. The honoured names of Haddington and of the Bairds of Newbyth—the great saddle of Tippoo Sahib is still a family heirloom, relic of a day when families were still proud of producing empire-builders—are in another sphere matched by the names of George Rennie of Phantassie, Robert Hope of Fenton and John Brodie of Scoughall, to say nothing of the generations of the Howdens of Lawhead. Andrew Howden, perhaps, who died in 1879, is outstanding among the great farmers of East Lothian, a commanding giant of a man who seems to have been able to talk on Shakespeare with as much ease and authority as on the management of crops.

Among the tall trees of the Tyninghame estate is a very lovely Norman arch, although the church of which it was part is now in ruins. It is the arch leading to the apse, now gone. There is another arch between nave and chancel, and an arched tomb-recess covering an effigy. The detail of arches and shafts and capitals is unusually sharp-cut and fine, and makes it possible to place the church in the twelfth century. There exists a charter of King Duncan II to the monks of St. Cuthbert at Durham, granting them "Tiningeham" and other places in the vicinity, no doubt because legend has it that Cuthbert was buried here. This was in 1094. However, there seem to be doubts about this document.

There is something English rather than Scottish about the comfortable rural beauty of this corner of the Lothians, and this is, or was, confirmed by the lovely church by the roadside a mile to the north. The burning down of Whitekirk must surely be the most wanton act of the entire Suffragette campaign—the senseless destruction of what must have been one of the choicest little churches in all Scotland. It happened in 1914. Since then the church has been superbly re-built, but there are things which cannot be restored. A strong, square tower with a pyramidal steeple rises above the junction of aisle, chancel and transepts, and there is a deep porch on the south side of the nave, a porch with diagonal buttresses typical of the fifteenth century to which the church belonged. The stonework is of a pinkish ashlar which marries happily into the greenery around, and when an autumn sun turns the pink to peach and gold and the big roadside trees throw violet shadows across the fields Whitekirk wears an air of ancient rural grace rarely found in Scotland. A somewhat biased and evidently post-Reformation document in the Vatican Library has a picturesque account of the origins of the church. It describes how men of the Scots army defeated by Edward I at Dunbar in 1294 shut themselves in Dunbar Castle then in the possession of Black Agnes, Countess of Dunbar, and proceeds to say that Black Agnes tried to escape to Fife, was injured, came ashore at Fairknowe, and there drank of a holy well which cured her, as a result of which she built a chapel and endowed it. The siege of Dunbar, successfully resisted by Black Agnes, happened forty years later. The document, however, records that the growing repute of the well caused a shrine to be built in 1309, to which no fewer than 15,653 pilgrims came a hundred years later, so that James I took the Chapel of Fairknowe under his protection, added to it and called it the White Chapel, dependant on his own Abbey of the Holy Cross in Edinburgh. Finally, the document declares, in the course of the Reformation, lands and offerings were seized, the shrine was " beat to pieces " by the reformers and " that Holy Chapell . . . was made a parochial church . . . and by them called Whitekirk." As the Royal Commission soberly objects in its survey of the monuments of East Lothian, Fordun calls it *alba ecclesia* in 1385 or thereabouts and the records of James IV's visits to it in 1491 and 1497 speak of " the Quhyt Kirk," so the name is old enough, if it was known also as Fairknowe and even Hamer, which is the old name for this part of the parish. That it was a great centre for pilgrimage is undoubtedly true. A pilgrim who came in 1435 was Æneas Sylvius Piccolomini, later Pope Pius II. Fulfilling a vow made at sea on his way to Scotland, the sort of vow, perhaps, which others before and since have made in certain circumstances—he made a barefoot pilgrimage over frozen ground to the shrine nearest his port of landing, which cannot have been nearer than Dunbar, and, catching a bad chill, had to be borne back in a litter. He later blamed his life-long rheumatism on his wintry pilgrimage to Whitekirk.

The Dunbar of Æneas Sylvius's day is gone, and there is not much left of the place as Black Agnes knew it. It is now a sprawling town of several thousand inhabitants, in the dawn or dusk from the window of a main-line London-to-Edinburgh express looking like an upraised, weathered outcrop of the Old Red Sandstone on which, and of which, it is built. A good deal of Scotland is built of the Old Red Sandstone. Transported from its setting—for example, to erect tenements among the soot and fog of Glasgow—it is a peculiarly unsympathetic and distressing material, weathering to a murky brown, killing other colours and blunting the effect of architectural detail ; but when used where it has been quarried, as at Dunbar, it may blend with the landscape or emphasise its features and reveal character which is hidden in alien surroundings. At least it shows up sharply the tawdriness of the average brick-and-harl council housing scheme as met with in south-east Scotland. Pre-1914 Dunbar is consistently Old Red, from the church steeples to the harbour works. Not that it was always a red town. In the seventeenth and eighteenth centuries many of the houses were probably rough-cast and whitewashed, as the Town House remained as late as the first decade or two of the present century, and it is perhaps a pity that the Town House and some other buildings in the High Street have not been restored to this condition, for the sake of its gay effect and the attractive contrast which it would make with the red freestone fronts and gables. The High Street is wide, and must once have had a rather Continental air. Probably its width was reduced by projecting shops like the Luckenbooths which used to jut into Edinburgh's High Street, and the Town House itself retained projecting booths or shops of a sort until quite recently. The Town House is fairly typical of a Scottish east-coast burgh. Its main feature is a bold, hexagonal tower relieved by string-courses and topped by a little spire. The only unusual thing about the building is the crowsteps on the gables, which are fitted with coping-stones, or " gabletted." Both clocks and sundials are mounted in the tower. Again as in Edinburgh, narrow closes or alleys break the length of the High Street, and many a Scot retains as his first holiday memory the salt tang of the sea and the cackle of quarrelling gulls coming up the closes of Dunbar. It is an old town, and pleasant on a warm summer day, but in the town itself there is not much else of special note except the monument to George Hume, Earl of Dunbar, in the parish church, a nineteenth-century building replacing an earlier church. The Earl died in 1611 and the monument, an elaborate Renaissance work probably by a foreign craftsman, is perhaps a little later in date. Dunbar was both Lord High Treasurer of Scotland and Chancellor of the Exchequer in England. He was also a chief instrument of the notorious " Jeddart justice " which brought order to the unruly Borders. And—ironically !—it was through him that James VI worked to defeat the Kirk.

To-day, the principal industry of Dunbar is no doubt the summer tourist traffic. If its claim to have the lowest rainfall in Scotland may sometimes be disputed by such other towns as Forres, in Morayshire, it is certainly true that downpours afflicting Edinburgh often pass by Dunbar, although the bitter winter winds there make one feel for Æneas Sylvius. The two inns recorded in the *Statistical Account* of 1845 have become a multiplicity of hotels and boarding-houses and purveyors of " bed-and-breakfast," but I have no knowledge as to whether contemporary Dunbar can compete with the " forty-six licensed ale-houses where low-priced spirits are retailed, and where the execrable custom of dram-drinking is practised," against which the writer of 1845 thundered, ending his denunciation with : " This we may justly pronounce to be the bane of all good and the source of all evil—the ruin of health and morals—and of all domestic duty and comfort—the reproach of man, and the disgrace of woman." The cheap liquor, incidentally, does not seem to have depressed the morals of Dunbar too heavily, since we read " The jail is in a very bad condition, and has been legally condemned ; but fortunately it is seldom occupied." At one time there was good reason for the liquor being cheap, as the town had considerable brewing and distilling industries. Flax and cotton milling were tried in the district, but the sea and the land and the marketing of their harvests are the traditional callings of the burgh. In the old days the herring fisheries were important, and the tale of the Lost Drave of Dunbar in the sixteenth century records how a thousand boats were seen setting their nets off the town one Sabbath morning, as result of which flouting of the minister's reproaches a great storm arose and destroyed 170 boats. Even a century ago as many as three hundred boats sometimes came in the late summer. All that, however, has gone. But the background prosperity of the district remains broad-based on the fine farming tradition, brought to perfection hereabouts on the well-drained light red loams.

Historically, the focal point of Dunbar is the desolately ruinous outline of the castle rising to blot out the sea behind the solid-built sandstone basin of the new harbour. So utterly are the ruins demolished that, at a casual glance, they might be storm-shattered pieces of the coast itself. The foundation of the castle is an eighty-foot rock-mass three parts surrounded by the sea, a natural strong-point which may perhaps be the reason for the name of Dunbar : *dun* being a hill in Gaelic, and *bar* a fortress. The place provides the only good natural haven between Berwick and the ports within the Firth itself. For an invader, it is the sea-gate of Lothian, and must therefore have been a defence-point since early times. It is hard to say now what the castle looked like : to deliberate destruction in historic times was added the blasting of an entrance to the new harbour through the heart of the old fortress mass, and crashing seas every winter have torn the masonry from the rocks piece by piece, solidly as the local freestone has clung there, cemented by locally-quarried lime. There is constant crumbling, and a great deal of the castle must have slipped into the seas which cavern the rocks below, even since the title-page view appeared in Miller's *The History of Dunbar* about a hundred years ago.

The castle has been laid in ruins several times. The existing ruins seem in the main to be those of James IV's reconstruction at the end of the fifteenth century, when war with England found the Lothians vulnerable. The task of building took four or five years. The Lord High Treasurer's Accounts—that invaluable Scottish source of information—contain picturesque details of the construction—*yettis* and *crukis* of iron, *dowbil byspikers* and *gret wraklin nalis*. The previous castle had been " cassyne doune and alutterly distroyit" by Parliament in 1488, because the English and their friends in Scotland had used it as a spearhead of the attack on Scotland, and because it was, so it would seem, impregnable. But it had not always been on the English side. In 1338 it was besieged by a great English army led by men who were to distinguish themselves at Crécy and Poitiers, chief among them Montacute, Earl of Salisbury. The master of the castle, the Earl of Dunbar, was elsewhere ; but Black Agnes, his countess, was at home and took charge of the defence. Clad in mail—according to one fanciful account—she exhorted the defenders, standing boldly on the battlements in full view of the enemy and, whenever the stone from a ballist splintered the rampart, she instructed a maiden in rich clothes to dust the place with a kerchief. When the English commander ordered up an engine called the Sow to shield his sappers whilst they dug a mine under the walls, Black Agnes, in a much-quoted if not very successful rhyming couplet, warned Montacute that his Sow would farrow and then had her men tip a vast boulder on to the engine so that the unfortunate sappers were obliterated or fled from under their shield. She even captured some of the besiegers by allowing them to think they had bribed a porter to let them in by night. The portcullis was dropped just too soon to catch Montacute himself, but his armour-bearer was trapped. Finally, the siege

was raised by Sir Alexander Ramsay, who sailed from the Bass
Rock with forty chosen men, eluded the big Genoese galleys of
the blockading fleet, and entering the castle by a sea-postern
brought food and new heart to the garrison. Ramsay rushed the
English next morning, withdrew and returned to the Bass by the
way he had come ; but the besiegers could not face another fruit-
less six weeks and called off the siege.

There is some obscurity about what happened to the castle
in the sixteenth century. By 1558 it seems to have been thought
vulnerable to gunfire, although not so long before John, Duke
of Albany, had equipped it well with " artaillze pulder and bullat-
tis." The French reinforced it in 1560 ; but it would seem they
only increased its capacity by some sort of outworks, for the
destruction of "the new buildings " ordered by the Treaty of
Leith later that same year made the castle in no way untenable.
It was a Royal castle, and Mary Queen of Scots made considerable use of it. She spent the Christmas of 1562 there. When the
Earl of Moray tried to destroy Lord Gordon, heir to the shattered
house of Huntly, by having him hung and quartered, Mary
caused the young man to be carried to Dunbar instead ; and
although Moray tricked Mary into signing a death-warrant the
Captain of Dunbar wisely doubted the warrant until he heard
the sentence from the Queen's own lips, and on being shown it
the Queen in horror tore up the paper and Gordon was released
later to become the Earl of Huntly. It was at Dunbar, again, that
Mary stayed when the rumour went about in 1564 that she might
try to fly to France. It was to Dunbar that she fled after the
murder of Rizzio in 1566, and it was from there that she tried to
avenge her favourite by issuing the proclamation raising the
country against the associated lords who had done the deed.
Then came the final phase of Mary's life, likewise in part enacted
at Dunbar. We have seen that Mary and Bothwell, after their
marriage, found refuge in Borthwick, and that Mary, garbed as a
page, followed her sinister third husband to Dunbar. The associated lords retorted by proclaiming that the Earl of Bothwell had
" put violent hands on the queen's person, and shut her up in the
castle of Dunbar." Here she mustered 4000 men, but elected to
march them to Carberry Hill and the defeat that was followed
by her surrender. It has been said that if she had stayed safely

within the walls of the castle the lords, without guns or siege
engines, would have been baffled. History might have taken a
different course. Likewise, Bothwell, if he had defied his enemies
from its ramparts instead of trying to fly to Orkney, would at
least not have ended his days in a Danish dungeon. The castle
itself held out for a little longer, but the Regent Moray mustered
an army in Edinburgh, with "four of the best double cannon,"
and this last persuasive argument caused the captain of Dunbar
to submit ; so that in far-off England the great Cecil was able
to write to the English ambassador in France "All things be
quiet in Scotland since the last of September, at which time the
castle of Dunbar was surrendered to the Earl of Murray." For
this great fortress was one of the keys to Scotland. In 1567 an
Act of James VI states " Our soverene Lord . . . hes ordainit, and
ordainis, that the castell of Dunbar and the forth of Inchekeith
be demolischit and cassin downe utterlie to the ground, and
distroyit in sic wyse that na foundment thairof be occasioun to
big thairupon in tyme cumming."

Between Dunbar and the White Sands lies the park of Broxmouth. In the park is a hillock called Cromwell's Mound. On
this grassy knoll the fate of Britain was decided one morning
about a century after Dunbar castle was reduced to ruin. On to
it Cromwell stepped to watch the Scots army that threatened him,
and never was the Protector of England nearer to defeat and its
consequences than on that September morning in 1650. Leslie,
the veteran Scots commander, experienced in continental wars,
had foiled Cromwell again and again until the Protector's troops
were in desperate case from sickness and starvation and weariness
of the spirit. Leslie had forced Cromwell back step by step
through the Lothians until he had him trapped at Dunbar—
trapped because the Scot had cut off his retreat to Berwick, in
Cromwell's own words, " by sending a considerable party to the
strait pass at Copperspeth (Cockburnspath), where ten men to
hinder are better than forty to make their way." The Scots vastly
outnumbered the Ironsides. Looking up at them in their commanding position on the Doon Hill, Cromwell must have come
as near as he ever did to despair. What he did not know was that
the power had been taken out of Leslie's hands and that the
Scots army was now commanded virtually by a committee of

zealot ministers, who forced their prudent general to leave his position of advantage. More than that, they had already purged the Scots army of "four thousand profane persons and Sabbath-breakers," which probably included the toughest soldiers and the veterans of Gustavus Adolphus's wars. All night the committee of ministers wrestled with the Lord in prayer, and believed the Lord had delivered Agag into their hands. But when Cromwell saw them all coming down off the Doon Hill it was his turn to mutter "The Lord hath delivered them into my hand," and when the sun cleared the haar steaming in off the sea behind him he cried "Now let God arise and his enemies shall be scattered." The Scots found themselves wedged between Doon Hill, the ravine of the Spott burn, and Cromwell's army, without room to manoeuvre. At first they withstood the attack and Lambert and Monk were both thrown back ; but when Cromwell himself brought up three regiments of foot and a body of horse, the Scots broke, and in the long retreat that followed they lost 3000 men killed and 10,000 prisoners, to a handful of English casualties. The victory of Dunbar gave Scotland to Cromwell.

It is not surprising that East Lothian has been both a battle-ground and the very birthplace of the Reformed religion, for rich as its fields are their virtues are only to be got at by hard labour in the face of all sorts of climatic odds, as we have seen earlier in this chapter. To plough those heavy fields in a wet spring with the peewits crying between the blasts of harsh nor' easter, even more to plant them with potatoes in a chill rain that makes miry channels of the drills, is a grim act of faith that moulds a man's beliefs into violent, dramatic shapes. It is hardly surprising, then, in the kirkyard of Morham, to come on old tombstones of the family of Knox which farmed the lands of Mainshill in the same parish. The farmhouse of Mainshill has long since disappeared, but a local tradition at one time enshrined the knowe where it stood as John Knox's place of birth. However difficult such traditions may be to substantiate, they are often well founded. Knox says in his *History*, recording a talk with Bothwell : "My grandsire, goodsire and father have served your Lordship's predecessors, and some of them have died under their standards." This could mean that Knox's forebears were tenants of the Bothwells, and we know that the Bothwells' Gifford estates included the lands of Mainshill. We know too that Knox's mother was a Sinclair of Northrig, and that Northrig was part of the Gifford estates. This meaning of " Gifford " is good enough to explain Buchanan's " Gifford in Lothian " as Knox's birthplace, or Beza's *Giffordiensis*. The commemorative stone set up by Carlyle in the Giffordgate of Haddington in fact seems to be misplaced. The *Statistical Account*, compiled as it was by parish ministers, each in the light of his own prejudices, actually claims both Haddington and Gifford as the birthplace within the same volume !

The reforming spirit welled up powerfully in another man whom tradition links with East Lothian. Sir David Lyndsay of the Mount is usually taken as a Fifer and certainly he had his higher schooling at St. Andrews University, but there is a persistent belief that he was born in the little castle of Garleton, among the long, low folds of the Garleton Hills. Whether those crumbling ruins are quite old enough to have seen this event, late in the fifteenth century, is in doubt ; but there seems to be no doubt the Lyndsays had their roots in the lands of Garmylton-Alexander, or Garleton, and sasine of them went to David Lyndsay de Mountht in 1478. Lyndsay's satire most certainly has an earthy Lothian quality, like Knox's rhetoric, and Lyndsay mocked his king just as Knox did his queen. Indeed, it has been said that the satiric verse of Lyndsay did more to further the Reformation than all Knox's sermons, this in spite of the fact that the poet died before the Reformation came about. He was a poet of the people, as Burns was to be three centuries after. Like Burns's, his influence did not die with him. How powerful that influence must have been was brilliantly demonstrated at the Edinburgh Festival, when *Ane Pleasant Satyre of the Thrie Estaits* was staged by Tyrone Guthrie in—most appropriately—the General Assembly Hall of the Church of Scotland. The rugged, coarse humour and the gorgeous characterisation is often Chaucerian and betrays the Anglo-Saxon impact which marked the Lothians more than any other region of Scotland.

The very name of Athelstaneford has an almost comically Saxon sound in Scottish ears. The story that Athelstan's body is buried by a ford over the Cogtail Burn is, or course, nonsense.

It is true that the *Anglo-Saxon Chronicle* says, under the year A. D. 934, that "King Athelstan went into Scotland, both with a land-force and a naval armament, and laid waste a great part of it"; but a page or two later it records the king's death at Gloucester in 941. The very village of Athelstaneford has a certain English look about it, not in the details of its cottages, but in its trimness and rural prettiness, although it has a high and windy prospect across the Firth to the far, blue line of the Highland hills. This high parish as a whole must have been populated since early times. The Garleton Hills are dotted with ancient forts. The finest of them, the Chesters, is on a small hill-top under a mile from Drem. Its five encircling ramparts are still clearly marked, and so are the hut-circles inside the fortifications.

Lyndsay's may be the greatest literary name associated with this secluded parish, but it is by no means the only one. Of the others, one, strangely enough, has shared with Lyndsay the distinction of a revival at the Edinburgh Festival. More, those two are the only old Scots works which have received major productions at the Festival unless we include the midnight performances of Ramsay's *The Gentle Shepherd*. John Home's *Douglas*, however, had not the success of Lyndsay's work. In spite of Dame Sybil Thorndike and a brilliant cast the lines could not be brought to life, although first Peg Woffington and then Mrs. Siddons herself took part in productions at Covent Garden. Home himself is more interesting than his plays. His connection with Athelstaneford was as minister of the parish from 1747 to 1757; but he had fought against the Jacobites at Falkirk, been taken prisoner and escaped, and when he resigned his parish owing to the objections of the Presbytery of Edinburgh to his adventures in the theatre world, he became secretary to the great Lord Bute, then tutor to the Prince of Wales and, at the age of 56 joined a regiment raised by the Duke of Buccleuch, only to injure his head by a fall from his horse. His predecessor as parish minister of Athelstaneford, the Rev. Robert Blair, indulged in no such colourful career, but he was probably the greater poet of the two. *The Grave* is scarcely the sort of title which would bring success to-day, but it brought Blair wide repute in eighteenth-century Scotland; and not in Scotland or in

The ruins of Dunbar Castle at the entrance to the modern harbour

his own time only, for the edition of 1808 is illustrated by
William Blake. Blair is buried in the kirkyard of Athelstaneford.
But the annals of this parish are meaty through and through,
salted with wit and character and richly crusted with achievement ranging from high renown to the sort of repute which
would have given joy to Burns. At the one extreme there are
the son of Blair, who became Lord President of the Court of
Session, and Sir John Hepburn, who died a Marshal of France at
the early age of 38 ; at the other are the droll farmer, Adam
Skirving, and Naysmith Simpson, a notorious schoolmaster.
Adam Skirving's fame hangs chiefly on the often-recounted
incident of the verse in which he taunted with cowardice a
certain Lieut. Smith of Cope's dragoons at Prestonpans. Smith
sent his second with a challenge, but the canny farmer retorted :
" Gang awa' back and tell Mr. Smith that I hinna time to come
to Haddington to gie him satisfaction ; but say if he likes to
come to Garleton I'll tak' a look at him, and if I think I'm fit to
fecht him, I'll fecht him, an' if no', I'll just do as he did—I'll rin
awa'." Rather less credible is the story said to be recorded by
three large stones by the road above Clackmae, for it has been
said they mark the spot where Adam Skirving achieved the
supra-Olympic record for the hop, step and jump of 61 ft. 6 ins !
Naysmith Simpson is best remembered by his will, which left
careful provision for the mourners who accompanied the hearse
from Haddington to Lyne and back to be refreshed at every
tavern on the way.

Haddington is the county town of East Lothian, until quite
recently called Haddingtonshire. It is an old town. It is full of
the unassertive beauty which belongs to Scots burgh architecture,
a beauty which is like old cheese or old wine in that it cannot be
savoured fully without familiarity and knowledge. And like
an old woman who is still beautiful, Haddington can take credit
for it. She shares with Crail across the Firth the distinction, rather
rare in Scotland, of having civic pride enough to make real
efforts to preserve her beauty. The town lies spread on low
ground in a bend of the River Tyne, and by good fortune the
right-angled bend from the High Street into narrow Hardgate
Street was an impossible obstacle to the never-ceasing, fast, heavy
traffic between Edinburgh and the south, and a by-pass was

The hexagonal tower of Dunbar's Town House

constructed to avoid the town, leaving it to conduct its life at a gentler tempo. Hundreds of tourists pass it by every summer, therefore, seeing nothing of it but the pale, sleepy reek from its chimneys with maybe a glimpse of the tower of the old church.

The High Street is a fine, wide street, though varying in its width like a natural waterway, and even splitting in two. Many of the houses clustering against it are of the seventeenth century, although modernised, and one at least has a lintel with a sixteenth-century date. Where the High Street meets the Hardgate and the Sidegate there are clusters of old buildings backed by the broad, placid stream of the Tyne, crossed by the lovely bridge which connects the town with the old suburb of Nungate. Well above the river is the red stone pile of the parish church of St. Mary the Virgin, partly roofless, but with walls intact enough to carry a new roof, a glorious fifteenth-century monument English in style, but with a Scots accent in its heavy-mullioned west window. It is still popularly called the Lamp of Lothian, although that title belongs to a lost church of the Franciscans, the very site of which is not known. Five centuries ago it contained no fewer than eleven altars, the names of some of which suggest the variety of human tides that have flowed through Lothian : the Haly Blude Altar, St. Towbart's Altar, Crispin and Crispianus, the Three Kings of Cologne. On the north wall of the revestry is a fine Renaissance marble monument to the Maitlands of Lauderdale which once carried verses written by James VI in praise of his Chancellor. His grandson, Charles II, raised another member of the family, John, Duke of Lauderdale, to the position of his favourite and most trusted counsellor. This bitter enemy of the Scots was born at Lethington, only a mile or two from this monument, a house connected with another but very different sort of favourite of Charles, as we shall see presently. Lauderdale, beginning his career as a man of the Covenant, ended by persecuting the Covenanters and seeking the downfall of any who opposed the supremacy of Crown over Church and State. For a long time he was the most powerful member of the notorious Cabal, as he above all others had the ear of the king. Now he lies in the vault under this monument in the parish kirk of Haddington. The long memory of the Scots for such religious persecution is illustrated by the incident of the old crone who, nearly a century and a half after Lauderdale's death was seen to grip the iron bars of his tomb, gibbering with fury. " What ails ye, gudewife ? " she was asked. " It's the Duke of Lauderdale," she replied. " Eh, if I could win at him I wud rax the banes o' him." The story that his guilt would not allow him to rest even in his tomb followed a discovery that the lead coffin did mysteriously move from one part of the vault to another, but the cold fact of the matter proved to be that the flood-waters of the nearby River Tyne at intervals found a way into the vault !

The most interesting of Haddington's old houses was the so-called Bothwell Castle, rising from the left bank of the Tyne, but more familiar from its round tower on the Dunbar road. Fifty years ago this was one of the best pieces of burgh architecture in Scotland, but early in this century it was allowed to become ruinous. It was a typical country gentleman's town house, though a good deal of imagination is now needed to render it impressive again, and in the sixteenth century it belonged to one Cockburn of Sandybed. Bothwell's name is linked with it because he took refuge in it when Arran and Moray were seeking him. He changed clothes with a woman turnspit in its vaulted kitchen, and in reward for his escape granted Cockburn and his heirs an annual award of twelve bolls of grain.

Haddington lies athwart the Lothian invasion route into Scotland, and has suffered by it. As early as the twelfth century it had a royal palace, and the true old Lamp of Lothian, according to Bellenden, must have been a glorious church. The town, however, was almost entirely built of wood in the old days. So often was it burned that it is astonishing how the inhabitants had the heart to rebuild. It was destroyed first in 1216 by King John, then again in 1244, and the following century by Edward III during the notorious " Burnt Candlemas." Hotspur in company with the Earl of Dunbar revenged themselves in 1388 on Haddington for a failure to take Hailes Castle. Again the town suffered when Henry VIII tried to betroth his son to Mary Queen of Scots by force, sending Hertford north with an army which laid waste East Lothian, and in 1548 the English seized and fortified it, in defiance of the capital only a day's march away. Earthworks and ditches seem to have been their first defences, with gun positions and fascines for the arquebusiers, making a position so strong that it resisted the Scots and their allies from France for more than two years. So often did wars sway back and forth over Haddington that at one time it was nearly impossible to dig the soil deeply without coming on human remains. And flood alternated with fire. The Tyne is a shallow stream, and heavy downpours in the Lammermuirs fill it rapidly. On Christmas eve of 1358 there was such an inundation that tall oaks were dragged up by the roots and carried seaward, and only when a nun in the abbey of Haddington seized a statue of the Virgin and threatened to throw it in the waters if they did not spare her abbey did the flood subside. On the festival of St. Ninian in 1421 constant rain so raised the level of the river that people had to go to church by boat, while the fine library of the sacristy was severely damaged. The greatest of all floods came in 1775, when the Tyne rose seventeen feet in less than an hour and half the town was flooded, with the whole of the Nungate, although no life was lost.

Haddington is essentially a county town, a rural centre, a market for the villages and farms of the rich country around. Once it had the greatest corn-market in Scotland, and the smell of grain-bags and hay, of sheep and flour-dust, still seems to be the smell appropriate to its wide, simple High Street, as to its narrow lanes near the river. No industries to speak of have intruded to jar the old way of life from its placid prosperity. In the churchyard is buried the only man who ever made Haddington widely noted as a manufacturing place, and as he met a sensational end the story of him is perhaps worth telling in full.

Sir William Stanfield was an Englishman who owned a property called New Mills, close to Haddington, in the reign of Charles II. The contrast between the poverty of the northern half of the United Kingdom and the wealth of the southern was already causing concern enough in high places to bring about attempts to put Scottish industries on a firmer footing. During his visit of 1681 the Duke of York himself took an interest in the possibilities of cloth manufacture, and a company was promoted by Stanfield and by Robert Blackwood, an Edinburgh merchant who a few years later was to be one of the directors of the Darien Company. New Mills was chosen as the site of the cloth manufactory. With the Lammermuirs behind it, there were plentiful supplies of wool, nearby Haddington could provide labour and provisions and, as market for the cloth, Edinburgh was within sight. For a moderate rental Stanfield leased his mills and "his office-houses, which are many, great and spacious." A capital of £60,000 Scots (£5000 sterling) was subscribed, enough to set up 20 looms and employ 233 hands. Like other enterprises of the kind at this time, the company was to be protected by Act of Parliament from imports from the south, although in no sense a monopoly, as other cloth companies were encouraged to go ahead until Scotland became self-supporting in the making of broadcloth. Scotsmen, indeed, were exhorted to be patriotic and "buy Scots," even although the cloth should be "a little dear at first" because of capital costs and "the many losses and inconveniences attending beginners."

It is seldom we have the chance to watch in such detail the progress and affairs of a business concern so far off in time as almost three centuries; but the minute-books of the New Mills Cloth Manufactory are preserved in the library of Edinburgh University and have been published by the Scottish History Society. The company had reasonable success for twenty years and more. Demand was heavy. In two years the number of looms had risen to twenty-five for cloth, and two for serges, and ten more looms were added to this number. In 1683 there were hopes of a big Government contract for soldiers' uniforms, for it seems that only now were such things coming into use in Scotland "to distinguish sojers from other skulking and vagrant persons," as the Privy Council put it. However, those hopes were not realised, and licences for the import of English cloth were issued which cut across the protection scheme under which the New Mills company had so far prospered. Then difficulties arose with the work people, partly over the imported labour on which the company relied to teach the men of Lothian their skills, and partly, one suspects, because the farm-bred men of the parish did not take kindly to serving the machines; but the imports of English and foreign cloth were the chief threat to the company, for the law was flouted constantly. This flouting culminated in the discovery that a member of the company itself, Councillor John Baillie, had brought in English cloth valued at

£400 sterling. He forfeited his stock in the company and the cloth was burned by the common hangman. The regulations were tightened up. The company prospered again for a time, and a monopoly of cloth for the army at last came its way, and we hear of such items as that the garrison of the Bass Rock had its uniforms made of New Mills cloth. In 1693 the company was incorporated by Act of Parliament and exempted from customs dues for twenty-one years, while in 1695 it was even exempted from taxation to offset the difficulties it had gone through. But the struggle began to go against the company at the beginning of the eighteenth century. Scottish woollen-manufacturers depended on cheap, plentiful home-produced wool, and when in 1704 an Act permitted the Scottish woolmasters to export all their wool, whether to England or the Continent, the Scottish manufacturers were dealt a heavy blow, redoubled by the English wool trade's determination to defend its prosperity by forcing the Scots and Irish to manufacture linen instead of wool. Some of the Scottish factories adapted themselves to the new difficulties, but not the New Mills company, and the mysterious death of Stanfield was one of the culminating blows. In 1713 machinery and plant were sold up, and the house and estate of New Mills went to a Colonel Charteris who—perhaps because of the sinister associations at the end—gave the place the name it retains to-day : Amisfield.

The grim case of Sir James Stanfield is summarised in a book referred to earlier in this chapter : *Fountainhall's Decisions*. The old judge describes how Stanfield was found dead near his home of New Mills. The Privy Council ordered two Edinburgh surgeons to inspect the body, and their report shows what a hybrid science forensic medicine was a mere two and a half centuries ago, for they record together signs of strangulation and also the grisly assertion that the corpse's head bled when Philip, the eldest son, touched it, and that thereupon "he let the body fall, and fled from it in the greatest consternation, crying 'Lord have mercy upon me !'" This is the last instance in a Scottish court of this old test being permitted, and the jury apparently took it seriously, for with little other direct evidence against him a verdict of guilty was brought in against Philip. It throws an interesting light on the times that this hard-headed

old Lothian judge should say of a case over which he had presided :
"This is a dark case of divination, to be remitted to the great
day whether he was guilty or innocent, only it is certain he was
a bad youth, and may serve as a beacon to all profligate persons."
Whatever the truth of the matter, the wretched Philip went to the
scaffold at the Cross of Edinburgh. His head was placed on a
spike on the east gate of Haddington, his body raised in chains
at the Gallow Lee, between Edinburgh and Leith. The whole
tale was set down and published in 1838 by a Haddington book-
seller, George Tait, under the dramatic title of *Philip Stanfield,
or the Parricide*.

As a source of literature, however, Haddington is no rival
to little Athelstaneford. Not that it is without associations with
the great. In the roofless choir of St. Mary's is a stone inscribed :

Here likewise rests JANE WELSH CARLYLE, Spouse of Thomas
Carlyle, Chelsea, London. She was born at Haddington, 14th
July 1801, only child of the above John Welsh and of Grace
Welsh, Caplegell, Dumfriesshire, his wife. In her bright
existence she had more sorrows than are common, but also
a soft invincibility, a capacity of discernment, and a noble
loyalty of heart which are rare. For forty years she was the
true and loving helpmate of her husband, and by act and
word unweariedly forwarded him as none else could in all of
worthy that he did or attempted. She died at London, 21st
April 1866, suddenly snatched from him, and the light of his
life as if gone out.

Not far off is the Georgian-style frontage of the house where
Thomas first met Jane's dark, inquiring eyes, and from which
she wrote her letters urging him to use his " precious time " and
"noble powers." Carlyle first came to this house and met his
future wife at the end of a seventeen-mile walk enforced on him
for his health's sake by his friend Edward Irving. Irving had
served as a dominie for three years in an upper room of the same
house, and Jane had been his favourite pupil—indeed the two
were for a time in love ; and he was to go on to be a great
preacher and missionary and finally the founder of the Catholic
Apostolic Church.

As Haddington has remained a market town, comfortably

presiding over its stretch of river as though trunk roads did not exist, so the southern part at least of the parish is stubbornly rural. Some of the very names themselves reek of a time when neither Press nor radio had taken the edge from the Scots tongue : Seggieshaugh, for example, or Dalgourie or, better, Barebanes and Duddybannets and—relics of the monkish farmers who gave the name to Monkrig—the fields called Upper and Lower Purgatory. There is a group of three old estates here : Coalstoun, Monkrig and Lennoxlove. The Brouns of Coalstoun seem to have been the oldest family in the parish, and the house is finely situated on high ground above the Coalstoun Water, to which the land falls in terraces which an eminent Scots judge, who in his cups had toppled over and rolled down them, mistook for the steps to the front door. There is fine timber on the estate, held in repute as early as the thirteenth century, and Coalstoun oak has gone into the hull of many a Scots ship. The chief family " treasure " is a curious wizened and mummified fruit reputed to be a pear given as a talisman by the Yester wizard, Hugo Gifford, to his daughter, and brought to Coalstoun by George Broun, who married a daughter of the third Lord Yester. Attempts to bite the pear, or even to dream of biting it, seem always to have been attended by unhappy consequences.

Another Hugo Gifford in the fourteenth century granted to Robert Maitland of Thirlestane the lands on which the neighbouring castle of Lennoxlove stands. It too looks across the Coalstoun Water. It rises grey and a little grim in the Scots baronial manner in the midst of fine, open parkland studded with stately trees a little over a mile to the south of Haddington, on the Gifford road. Its old name was Lethington Tower, and for more than three centuries the name of Maitland of Lethington had the ring of fame in Scottish annals. The core of the house is the fifteenth-century tower of rubble, with some sixteenth-century additions. The main block belongs to a time when a man's home no longer needed to be a fortress, for the Latin inscription over the entrance records that John Maitland, Earl of Lauderdale, carried out improvements in 1626, at the same time admitting the obscure origin of the tower—

QUIS TURRIM EXCITAVERIT INVIDA CELAVIT ANTIQUITAS

It was this tower itself around which so much history revolved. A document displayed in the ante-room carries the signature of the first of the great Maitlands, Sir Richard, who served a succession of sovereigns, as Jamie the Saxt himself acknowledged —" Our grandschir, gud sir, gud dam, muder and ourself being oftentymes employit in public charges, quhereof he dewtifullie and honestlie acquit himself." A carved stone coat-of-arms over the door in the banqueting-hall belongs to John Maitland, Lord Thirlestane, who wrought to establish the new kirk in Reformation times. The greatest of the Maitlands, William, died before his father and never succeeded to the property, and his only visible link with it is the avenue of limes and planes called in his honour the Politician's Walk. This was the great Secretary Maitland, singled out by Queen Elizabeth as " the flower of the wits of Scotland," and the story goes that he spent much time in thought strolling along this avenue. He was the staunch champion of Mary, Queen of Scots, and lost his life in her cause, although he cheated the execution block by dying in prison. The tower itself was several times besieged, notably by the invading English army under that Duke of Gloucester who, a year or two later, was to usurp the English throne as Richard III, and it was the headquarters of the Scottish army which, with the French, laid siege to Haddington in 1548.

The present owner of the house is the Duke of Hamilton, who bought it as recently as 1947. It contains, therefore, a fascinating and, at first sight, bewildering combination of Hamilton and Maitland possessions and relics. Only in a single item, a painting, do the two overlap. Over the mantelpiece in the White Room hangs a double portrait by Cornelis Janssen of the 2nd Duke of Hamilton standing beside John Maitland, 2nd Earl and 1st and sole Duke of Lauderdale—the notorious persecutor of the Covenanters whose tomb in St. Mary's, Haddington, has already been mentioned. He added a good deal to the house, probably carrying on his father's work, and built a wall right round the park with three great ports in it. In 1679 the Duke and Duchess of York made a royal progress northwards to Edinburgh and stayed a fortnight at Lethington, as it still was, where the retinue and company numbered as many as 2000.

In the drawing-room hangs a French portrait of a Hamilton

who, indirectly, shed some light on the change of the house's name from Lethington to Lennoxlove. It is of Count Anthony, a romancer and poet whose best-known work is the Memoirs of his rather disreputable but fascinating brother-in-law, the Comte de Grammont. The Memoirs form one of the most useful of all source-books on the scandals and tittle-tattle of the Court of Charles II ; but no evidence of those delicious scandals is more intriguing than the spectacular discovery made about the year 1900 in an attic of this Lothian mansion. This was a silver toilet-service, French work of about 1680 but probably finer than anything of the kind to have survived in France herself, now displayed in the Royal Scottish Museum in Edinburgh. It belonged originally to Frances Stewart, Duchess of Richmond and Lennox, called by Henrietta Maria, widow of Charles I, " the prettiest girl in the world," and by the notorious de Grammont " La Belle Stuart." Frances flits through the pages of many diaries and even of State papers of her time. " I fancied myself sporting with her with great pleasure," writes Pepys. " With her hat cocked and a red plume, sweet eye, little Roman nose and excellent *taille*, she is the greatest beauty I have ever seen." But she was not for Pepys. She came to Court under the wing of my Lady Castlemaine, the reigning mistress, and it was in her apartments that Charles himself found the young beauty ; and soon Pepys records " the King is now become besotted with Miss Stewart, getting her into corners," or, " the King dallies with her openly, and then privately in his chamber below." Frances was slender and graceful, she danced well, had the dress-sense given her by a French upbringing—had everything, in fact, except brains, for, wrote the Count Anthony Hamilton of the portrait, " it was hardly possible for a woman to have less wit or more beauty." But although she was a mere giggling girl playing hunt-the-slipper and building card-castles with my Lord Buckingham, she could break hearts. One suitor threw away his life in a sea-fight with the Dutch ; John Roettiers, who made her the model for Britannia on the new coinage, was deeply in love with her. And the King showered gifts on her, of which the magnificent treasure now in Edinburgh was perhaps the finest. Nell Gwynne's silver bedstead and Louise de Querouaille's massive plate, admired by John Evelyn, have long since disappeared ;

but Frances Stewart's toilet service lay safe under the cobwebs of this East Lothian attic. It was made in Paris, evidently specially for her, since each of the seventeen pieces comprising it bears her monogram several times over. The service was not a gift of the earlier days of the King's pursuit, for the monograms carry her coronet as Duchess of Richmond. She played the royal wooer with considerable skill, for under her frivolous exterior and her French airs and graces there lay a canny Scot. Maddened by frustration, Charles is said to have had thoughts of divorcing his Queen to put Frances in her place. But Frances instead ran away with the Duke of Richmond and, having made herself a "respectable" married woman, seems to have looked more kindly on the King's advances. Indeed, it may be he came nearer to loving her truly than he did any other woman, for even when the smallpox disfigured her at the early age of 21 he became more attached than ever, and it is probably to this time that the toilet service belongs.

Frances survived her husband by thirty years and her royal lover by seventeen. She was buried in Westminster Abbey, where there are preserved a little effigy of her and also her stuffed parrot! She left a considerable fortune. Apart from some annuities to her cats, this went to her cousin's son the fifth Lord Blantyre. With it her trustees in 1703 bought the estate of Lethington, and in accordance with her will they renamed the property Lennoxlove. This, not the romantic tale that Frances sent Blantyre the price of the purchase in a silver casket "with Lennox's love to Blantyre," is the true origin of the name. Several pieces of Frances' furniture are still to be seen there, and there are splendid portraits of herself and of her husband by Lely in the White Room.

The subsequent story of the great toilet service is perhaps scarcely relevant to this book, but I will add a few words on it, partly to explain why it is no longer at Lennoxlove, and partly because I had the good fortune to play a small part in it myself.

For many years the toilet service was lent by the then owner of Lennoxlove, Major Baird, to the Royal Scottish Museum. A few years after the Second World War it became necessary for the owner to sell it, and for the first time in two centuries it left the Lothians and lay in Messrs. Sotheby's rooms in London awaiting sale. It was an eagerly-awaited event and although the sale was to include also such celebrated lots as the Galloway Mazer, the service received the honour of having a catalogue to itself. The event was televised by the B.B.C. In approximately two minutes the bids rose to £17,000 and, amid cheers, the toilet service with the romantic story behind it was knocked down to the Museum and came back to a resting-place within a few miles of that Lennoxlove where it had lain so long.

CHAPTER THREE

The Lower Frith

THE WIDENING funnel of the Forth is near its mouth suddenly
nipped in to a span of a dozen miles between headlands. On the
Fife headland lies Elie, and on the opposite Lothian shore is a
rather similar sort of town, North Berwick. On the Lothian side,
therefore, the lower Frith of the Forth extends from North
Berwick westwards round a string of sandy bays backed by grassy
links to the grey clusters of chimneys and spires and grain
elevators which mark Leith and Granton. This coastal strip has a
character of its own. In a way, it belongs less with the rest of
the Lothians than it does with other such strips of dunes and grass
round the Scottish coasts—over in Fife, for example, in Angus,
in Ayrshire—a scene in which picturesque fishing villages, once
active but no longer so, alternate with large and prosperous-
looking golf-club houses presiding over superb fairways cut by
brown, purling burns crossed by little wooden bridges.

North Berwick is quite different from that other popular
watering-place, Dunbar, just round the corner of the coast. It
is an old town, too, an ancient royal burgh ; but Dunbar is lean
and weather-beaten where North Berwick hides its old bones in
a garment of expensive Victorian and Edwardian villas now
mostly seeking rejuvenation as hotels or as the more exclusive
sort of board-residences. Rather exclusive is something which
North Berwick has always been, and still contrives to be. For a
very accessible east-coast resort it preserves a quite remarkable
west-endyness. Gone perhaps are the days of local snobbery
when the caddies preferred Mr. A. J. Balfour of Whittinghame
to a Russian Grand Duke, and Margot Asquith and the Smart
Set no longer monopolise the first tee ; but the lower Frith
in general and North Berwick in particular are still in favour
with the die-hard core of Edinburgh society while to stay
in North Berwick and travel to and from theatres and concerts

in Edinburgh has become a habit with some of the more discriminating among Festival visitors. And—I had almost forgotten it!—where but at North Berwick would the England Fifteen limber up and prepare for the biennial Calcutta Cup struggle with Scotland at Murrayfield, thereby conferring on this watering-place apart a faint odour of that sanctity which invests Twickenham and Lords' and Wimbledon.

Yet even on the golf course the far-off past is present. On the West Course there is a cairn where a stone cist and bones and urns were found, and the *Proceedings of the Society of Antiquaries of Scotland* record a skeleton from a point fifty yards west of the 12th hole. There are, as one would expect, remains also on the great conical Law which rises to 640 feet behind the town, the hill from which the whinstone was quarried to build the town, topped with a whalebone arch which is a relic of the long-gone Dunbar whaling fleet. The most impressive remains in the town itself are the ruins of a Cistercian nunnery founded in the twelfth century by Duncan, Earl of Fife, with an obligation upon the nuns to receive all the poor folk and pilgrims whom they could accommodate. It was a prosperous foundation, with lands yielding revenue both in Lothian and in Fife. The pilgrims themselves no doubt brought money to the place, and a stone mould for making pilgrims' badges, one showing St. Andrew on his cross, was found in a nearby graveyard : the graveyard of the old kirk by the harbour, now gone but for one small building of no great interest in itself. This may well be the kirk associated with the case of the notorious "North Berwick Witches" accused of compassing the death of the king on the high seas. King Jamie took a great interest in the trial of Agnes Sampson who confessed to being present when the Devil preached in this very kirk to a congregation of witches and warlocks. They danced in the kirk-yard, a whole hundred of them, then went into the darkened church and "the Devil startit up himself in the pulpit like a muckle black man, and everyone answered 'Here'." They then proceeded to open up three graves—not perhaps so difficult, as the sea had been disintegrating the cemetery for hundreds of years—and took off fingers and toes by the joints, Agnes Sampson for her part getting "a winding sheet and two joints."

The country behind the Law is not remarkable, or even

especially beautiful to eyes other than the agriculturalist's : the same rolling, finely-farmed fields as one meets with at the back of Dunbar. The farms are prosperous, not picturesque. One of them, however, Gleghornie, occupies the site of a vanished village with the same name where the great John Major was born in 1470. It is small wonder that Scotland has been riven by theological controversy when three such fierce champions of the views which clashed in the Reformation, Knox, Lyndsay and Major, were born within a few miles of one another in this fertile corner of the Lothians. Major actually went to the same school as Knox was to do in Haddington, and for long it was believed he taught him in Glasgow ; but he was a staunch medievalist and an upholder of the older church. To him reform smelt of Lutheranism, and Lutheranism was plain heresy. But all Europe competed in praising him as a distinguished scholar, lauding him in the most extravagant language. His *History of Greater Britain* is outstanding for its learning. Knox himself records that Major was present to hear that first challenging sermon of his at St. Andrews, the sermon that " struck at the very roots " of established religion, but he says nothing of Major taking up the challenge. For all his travels and repute the great schoolman retained intimate memories of his young days near North Berwick, and his country taste for porridge and oatcakes drew upon him a well-known jibe from the pen of Rabelais.

As so often happens round the shores of Britain, there is marked contrast here between the rather dull, bucolic scenery inland and the challenging and romantic beauty of the coast. From green, rolling pastures and fat, red fields there is a sudden fall by cliff or cleugh to the sea. Passing south-east from North Berwick there is a series of greater or lesser bays which give the answer to the otherwise rather puzzling popularity of this bare coastline. Canty Bay is the best known, facing as it does the hump of the Bass Rock ; but only about a mile from John Major's birthplace a side road leads past a lodge down to a wooded dene and the sea lapping a magnificent sandy beach curving in a half-moon between headlands of dark, jagged rocks where the sea foams and surges green in cracks and chasms. Even the paper and broken bottles which have invaded the place since it became accessible to the motoring masses cannot destroy its loveliness. Rounding the north headland of the bay, one faces the sort of scene which inspired the best work of John Thomson of Duddingston—the ruinous towers of Tantallon Castle looming gigantic on their cliff-top through the pearly sea-haze of the intervening bay.

There is not a finer castle in Scotland than Tantallon. As castles go, it is a rather curious structure in that it really only has one side to it, the other " sides " being formed by 100-foot cliffs dropping sheer to the sea, therefore almost impregnable. The man-made castle consists of three powerful towers linked by a curtain wall sealing off the small promontory enclosed by the cliffs, and this formidable frontage is made even more difficult of assault by a deep ditch or moat cut in front of it, some part of it through the rock itself. The Mid Tower is also a gatehouse, and there were originally drawbridge and portcullis flanked by salient towers which overhung the drawbridge and must have enabled the defenders to concentrate a murderous fire of bolts, bullets, boiling oil or what you will on any force which succeeded in reaching the entrance. The Douglas and East Towers, at the ends of the wall, are of the same height as the Mid Tower, although they are now in such a state of ruin that the rooms inside are open to the winds. Under the Douglas Tower is a vaulted chamber known as the pit, which is complete with ventilation flue and a garderobe with soil flue. It would seem the defenders could maintain some sort of sea communication with their friends elsewhere, for a series of holes in a reef of rock on the shore below were apparently for posts supporting a jetty, and there are some remains on the cliff-top which may indicate the position of a crane. Water was drawn from a 100-foot well in the courtyard.

" Our castle of Temptaloun " is mentioned for the first time in 1374, when William, first Earl of Douglas and Mar, gives it as his address ; and the greater part of the existing structure belongs to this century. Over the next century a succession of notable men held the castle, including the Grim Douglas and Archibald " Bell-the-Cat," Earl of Angus, then it became a Royal castle and in 1452 was granted by James II to George Douglas, Earl of Angus. In 1528 James V had to lay siege to the place, and not

The Abbey Church at Haddington,
popularly called ' The Lamp of Lothian '

all his cannon, though he had two 8-inch pieces, could reduce the castle. When the King at last got the castle into his hands by coming to terms with the governor he took good care to strengthen it against the risks of even heavier ordnance by reinforcing with many tons of the green basalt blocks from the shore which can still be seen. Hertford, on his invasion of the Lothians in 1544, had a mind to lay siege to Tantallon, but thought better of it as he had neither heavy artillery nor powder enough. It was a powerful threat to the communications of any invader of the Lothians. Not only could its garrison sally forth by land and fall upon supply trains, but there was also a threat to shore-hugging supply vessels from the castle's guns " that wolde shote two mylys." It was gunpowder, however, which at last reduced the twelve-foot walls and gave the lie to the old Lothian phrase for the impossible—" Ding doon Tantallon, mak a brig to the Bass." In 1651 Monk with about 3000 of Cromwell's Ironsides lay before the outworks and began a systematic artillery bombardment. Two days' firing of *granadoes* (some kind of explosive shell) had small effect on the tremendous masonry ; but the English then brought up six " battering-pieces " which gradually made a large breach in the wall and also conveniently filled the ditch with rubble and stones. After this the castle was allowed to fall into further ruin. Yet oddly enough the siege of 1651 was not the last. Hugh Miller in his *Geology of the Bass* tells how in the early part of the nineteenth century a gang of thieves headed by a shipwrecked sailor took possession of Tantallon and used it as a base for descents on the neighbouring farms and mansions. A local *posse* eventually cornered the last of the gang in the Mid Tower, and John Rennie of Castleton, a huge farmer who used to amuse himself by throwing a 35-lb. stone about, climbed into the vaults and brought the robber out.

Like Gibraltar Rock, the Bass is a familiar shape to thousands who have never seen it, but the first sight of it rarely fails to impress, for it is a dramatic mass to come suddenly into sight from some woody lane around North Berwick. It is of course one of the strange volcanic plugs which have played such important parts in the story of the Lothians, relics cast enduringly in the fiery Carboniferous Age to give the unborn race of men places of vantage from which to dominate one another. What

The River Tyne at Haddington

the stranger is not prepared for is the stark whiteness of the cliffs. This is more marked at some times than at others; but when a lurid light comes off the sea against a thundery northern sky the precipices can seem spectral, with a movement about them like snow-flakes slowly moving in suspension, coming or going as they drift through bars of light. The snow-flakes are the sea-birds which nest in huge numbers on the Bass, the white cliffs are white with the droppings of countless generations of the birds. The Bass is sacred to ornithologists as one of the very few breeding stations of the gannet or solan goose, which even in the wildest gales can be seen soaring and plummeting like cannon-shot into the spuming waves of northern waters. The incubation period is in June and July, and this is the right time to see the Bass. Once there was a considerable trade in the birds, organised from Canty Bay, for the Scots considered them good eating and worthy of the table of the King. Twelve birds a year was one of the perquisites of the minister of North Berwick, as Vicar of the Bass. " A most delicate fowle " Taylor, the Water-Poet, calls it. " It is eaten in the form as wee eate oysters, standing at a side-boord, a little before dinner, unsanctified without grace; and after it is eaten, it must be well liquored with two or three good rowses of sherrie or canarie sacke." Not all visitors, however, agree with Taylor. After tasting it at a banquet Charles II is believed to have declared there were two things which he disliked in Scotland : solan goose and the Solemn League and Covenant. Taylor says the owner of the Bass made £200 a year by selling the birds. The young, tender birds only were taken, in July, by men let down on ropes from the cliff's edge. At one time an annual Bass dinner took place at Canty Bay, although so far as I can discover the main fare was not goose but legs of lamb contributed by the farmers who attended in large numbers. Bass mutton was prized in the Lothians in the days when a butcher's customers could be discriminating. The pasture, enriched with guano, made tender feeding ; but it is very limited in extent, and when an Edinburgh butcher made private boast that he sold a hundred Bass sheep every year he made it obvious that all was not Bass that bore the label.

The earliest-recorded owners of the island were the Lauders of the Bass, whose arms include a solan goose sitting on a rock.

Their tenure may have gone back as far as the reign of Malcolm Canmore. It lasted until Charles I—perhaps having more esteem for the geese than his son was to do!—claimed it as Royal property. The Merry Monarch had a grimmer use for it. He turned it into a prison for Presbyterian ministers, who were to be known as the Martyrs of the Bass. This chapter in the island's history is, indeed, one of the blackest things in the indictment against Lauderdale which drove the old woman to heap imprecations on his tomb in Haddington. He got himself made Captain of the Bass—which incidentally brought him a useful income from the sale of the geese—and used the dungeons of the island's fortifications for confining the staunchest men of that Covenant which his master bracketed with solan gooseflesh as twin objects of his dislike. About forty such prisoners were confined on the Rock over the years between 1672 and the Revolution of 1688, and many an old minister languished and died in the damp, smoky cells. The hatred which Lauderdale earned in his own county of Lothian was well-deserved. It serves to underline what an inexact science the writing of history is, and how there may be times when historians in their detachment cannot fully see the trees for the wood. The final chapter in the story of the Bass's use for Stewart ends—a little-known one—is its prolonged resistance to the forces of Dutch William, for this " small lonely isle " alone of all parts of the United Kingdom refused to recognise the new dynasty until 1694. Not only did the " loyalists " hold the island against all attacks, but they sallied at times against the coasts of Lothian and Fife. They were kept well supplied with provisions by sympathisers not only in Scotland but as far afield as France. When one of these was caught and a gallows erected on the shore opposite the Bass to hang him and dismay the defenders, the defenders scattered the executioners with cannon-balls. Later, they were starved out by warships ; but by regaling the Government's surrender-delegates with some fine fare and rich wine which they had saved they tricked them into offering terms which included their own lives ! The castle, once one of the strongest in Scotland, was destroyed after the surrender. Its ruins now look like some shattered pinnacles of the great Rock itself, and Thomson of Duddingston lent them a Wagnerian grandeur which they do possess under some conditions. It is said to have been accessible only by rope-ladder or by a bucket hauled up by chains, and something in the nature of a pulley-arm is certainly indicated in one early print. As at Tantallon, the " castle " was a wall across the lowest point of the Rock, the remaining defences being the precipices themselves. It was a French military expert who, according to Bishop Lesley, after inspecting a number of the great Scottish castles, declared he " had never sene in ony countrey so mony strengthis to natour, within ane prince's dominion." East Lothian has probably a heavier concentration of these fortresses than any other county. Only a mile or two westwards from North Berwick lies a castle which, in some ways, is the most formidable of the lot : Dirleton. Dirleton is not only formidable ; it looks all that a baronial stronghold should do, and with its walled pleasance, its dovecot, its fine trees and the enclosure which must once have been a bowling-green it has an air of the iron hand in the velvet glove which rarely lingers about the Scottish castle of early times. For Dirleton is early. A great deal of the original thirteenth-century masonry remains—pale, locally-quarried ashlar blocks set in ten-inch courses which are easily recognised. The remainder of the castle consists of fifteenth- and sixteenth-century restorations and additions. It looks a difficult place to capture, but medieval soldiers had their methods just as much as a modern general disposing of all the resources of technology, and the castle changed hands several times. It belonged in the first instance to one of the Norman families settled in the Lothians by David I, the De Vaux. Like the other great castles of the neighbourhood, it menaced the supply-lines of English invaders, and in 1298 Edward I sent the Bishop of Durham to reduce it, which he did after some difficulty, the castle remaining in English hands for many years. A De Vaux heiress brought it by marriage to the Halyburtons in the fourteenth century, and two centuries later a Halyburton heiress likewise conveyed it to the Ruthvens, later the Earls of Gowrie. Gowrie bribed Logan of Restalrig with it to take part in the Gowrie Conspiracy against King Jamie the Saxt, and Logan eagerly accepted for he thought it " the pleasantest dwelling-place in Scotland." When the plot failed, Jamie gave Dirleton to his rescuer, Sir Thomas Erskine. In 1650 it became a headquarters and hiding-place for the moss-troopers, but Monk made short work of the gate with mortar fire, and afterwards " demolished " the castle.

Dirleton village lies at the gates of its castle in the true medieval manner. Not that it is anything like as old as the castle, but it is old enough, and it is only a pity that the traffic of the Edinburgh-North Berwick road cuts through its seclusion. The central feature is a village green some 8 or 9 acres in extent, and the cottages with their brilliant gardens face upon this green, while a screen of great trees behind them gives privacy and shelter and perhaps a special climate of its own to the village. There are one or two inns, and lately a reputation for fine cuisine and excellent cellars has summer and winter brought a pilgrimage from Edinburgh of those hungering and thirsting for something a little different. The church tucked into the north-west corner of the village is just right in the circumstances. If not quite the medieval gem which it might have been in an English village of the same kind, its simple austerity has some of the same appeal as the Communion cups of the period, the early seventeenth century. There is a good late Gothic window at the south side of the aisle. The beauty of the place reflects the richness of the soil in this most northerly corner of the Lothians, as well as a long tale of good husbandry. It is said that the army of Edward I lived well off the pease and beans which they got from the fields around Dirleton and, as the Rev. Andrew Macgie wrote in 1627, " There is no occasion of lyming within the Lordship of Diriltoune, sicklyke ther growes noe sic quheate in all the toun of Goolan, Elbottle, and maist pairt of the College steid."

" Goolan " is of course that neighbouring village with the much-discussed name, Gullane. The generally-accepted pronunciation of the name to-day is *Gillan*, although one meets occasionally people who, either out of an apparent profundity of special knowledge or because they prefer to be thought a little different, call the place *Gullan*. The old name was Golyn, but I hesitate to go so far as one local writer of Victorian days who traces it back to " Golan in Bashan " in the twentieth chapter of Joshua ! The church apart, the old village has disappeared. One builds up from the records an engaging picture of it in its decline. In 1612 Parliament merged it in the parish of Dirleton on the grounds that it was " ane decaying toun, and Dirleton is

ane thriven place," while its last vicar evidently consoled himself
for a shrinking congregation by joining the increasing community of smokers, a "filthie habit" for which James VI,
perhaps with a glimpse of the rare foresight which he sometimes
revealed, deposed him from his office. The modern Gullane as
one passes through it on the main road is not particularly interesting, but there are many pretty enough villas hidden among the
trees on the seaward side, for the village not only fills with summer
visitors but is a dormitory for numbers of week-end refugees
from Edinburgh 18 miles away. The choicest corner of it is
around the ruined parish church, which disintegrated after the
ordinance of 1612, which included the complaint that the church
and churchyard were being "continewallie overblawin with
sand" and the direction that, if necessary, the materials of the
church were to be used for the building of Dirleton kirk. Gullane
church goes back in part to the second half of the twelfth century,
making it one of Scotland's oldest churches, and the chancel
arch is Norman work.

Gullane's fame to-day is founded principally on the cult of golf.
It lies very near the strategic centre of what is probably the
greatest concentration of first-class golf courses in the world, a
vast chain of links which, broken only here and there, stretches
from North Berwick to Leith. It has been developed enormously
in the past half-century. My Victorian author already quoted
says of Gullane : "The round is very extensive, consisting of
eighteen holes. The playing-ground is various, from a dead
level to a gradual ascent to the summit of the 'Whim', which
variations make it all the more interesting to experienced and
professional players, but irksome to young hands. When the
summit is reached a rest is perhaps necessary, and some inward
refreshment for some minutes, and to allow the golfer, new to
the ground, to view the splendid scenery." In these present days,
when the capital cost of equipping a golfer for the links must be
roughly comparable to the cost of equipping a soldier for an
extensive campaign, scenery is no doubt a regrettable distraction ;
but at least the golfer can claim that not even agricultural land
is half so sacrosanct and safe from the clutches of those strange
guardians of our liberties, the local authorities, as land required
for the ancient and royal game ; and so nothing has spoiled the

prospect of dunes and turf, of gulls wheeling against sea and sky, which gave delight to R. L. Stevenson in his memories of Gullane.

The great areas of golf links along the lower Frith, hereabouts merging one into another so that no one can point instantly to the bounds of Gullane or Luffness or Muirfield, are not only the sporting metropolis of the Lothians : they are of intense interest to the social historian. The bond between Scotland and the Low Countries is so strong and so multiple that the strands of it seem countless. It shows itself in big, obvious things such as our east-coast building styles and the words of the Scots speech, and in less obvious things like the bells and the brass chandeliers and the silver beaker Communion cups in our east-coast churches. But nothing in Scots tradition owes such a debt to the Dutch as the national cult of golf, and nothing owns to it more clearly than the location of the game in its earliest stages along this shore of the Lothians. We do not know if and when golf came from Holland to Scotland, but the bulk of the traffic between the two countries flowed into the Forth, and it was here mainly from the earliest times that immigrants settled and ideas took root. The Dutch sport was not played only on the frozen canals as so many of the paintings and old tiles seem to suggest, for an early sixteenth-century Book of Hours from Bruges, now in the British Museum, shows putting in progress towards a hole in the turf. The links stretching eastwards along the coast from Leith may well at an early stage have tempted homesick Hollanders to while away the summer evenings as they had been used to do at home. By the sixteenth century it had become an established sport of Scottish kings, and Mary is accused of playing golf with Bothwell at Seton, a little west of Gosford Bay, a few days after Darnley's death. By the seventeenth one imagines the whole stretch of the links alive with figures and echoing with the click of clubs, for James VI was so concerned at " the quantitie of gold and silver " going to Holland to pay for golf balls that he prohibited their importation. There were in those days of course no laid-out golf courses. The *Statistical Account* gives a merry picture of a great democratic pastime in which " all distinctions of rank were levelled by the joyous spirit of the game." Naturally the proximity of the capital city with its hordes of townsmen eager for exercise made those great stretches of seaside turf of the Lothian coast the cradle of the Scottish game, for your real countryman has usually other and more urgent things to do than the gratuitous propulsion of small balls into holes in the ground. Here was founded the world's first golf club. In 1744 "several Gentlemen of Honour, skilful in the ancient and healthful exercise of Golf," induced the City of Edinburgh to present a silver club to be played for annually over Leith Links. As the well-tried turf of Leith wore thin it ceased to be the central arena of the golfing world ; but the game's senior club, the Honourable Company of Edinburgh Golfers—not, be it noted, the Royal and Ancient Club of St. Andrews—in course of time moved eastwards a little and now has its home at Muirfield, near Gullane, the great championship course in the clubhouse of which the original silver club has been viewed respectfully by most of the world's leading players of modern times.

In Scotland, golf has never ceased to be a democratic sport, but her seaside links are extensive enough to accommodate everybody, and the coming of the clubs brought a certain exclusiveness which, if it put something of a damper on jollity, introduced some new, picturesque notes. There was, for instance, a colourful ritual by the nineteenth century. Perhaps North Berwick led the way in this. In 1832 its club was formed " of noblemen and gentlemen from all parts of the country." The *Statistical Account* records that "the number of members is limited to 50, who are admitted by ballot ; one black ball excludes, and the ballot must take place in the rotation of nomination 'before going to dinner '." Dinners counted for much at North Berwick, as the Rev. John Kerr relates, members vying with one another in the choiceness of their contributions, and we find the Bass mutton mentioned earlier in this chapter competing with grouse from Whittinghame and more exotic fare such as *gâteau napolitain* and "Perigord pie," whatever that may be. The uniforms so rigidly insisted upon likewise contributed to the pattern of the cult. All the way from North Berwick to Musselburgh a hundred years ago the red coats and toppers were to be seen dappling the green turf laced with drifts of golden sand. Not all the massed galleries which have watched the late " Babe " Zaharias win the British Ladies Championship at Gullane or, at Muirfield, saw the British Curtis Cup team achieve their only victory over the Americans, will quite make up for the passing of absurd but solemn rituals.

Passing westwards from Gullane, the main road runs the gauntlet of a fomidable concentration of golf courses. The three Gullane courses give place to Luffness on the left, then comes Aberlady Bay, once the port for Haddington and the refuge for the fishing fleet, but even the vessel is gone whose ribs used for so long to project gruesomely from the shore at low tide like the background to Holman Hunt's picture of the scapegoat. In place of the boat's ribs linger some of those depressing concrete anti-tank defences which in some parts of the coast it seems to have been nobody's business to remove. No doubt the long tidal flats of Aberlady Bay were always attractive to invading fleets, and the men from over the eastern sea must often have leaped overboard and stormed ashore to pillage the rich farms inland. Now the sea-flats are mainly tenanted by duck and other such aquatic fowl. Strangely enough, for all its sheltered look and its shallow bays, this is a heavily eroded coastline. All the way round from North Berwick to Aberlady and even much farther up the Firth, land has gone under to the sea's attacks. Geikie wrote that since Maitland in his *History of Edinburgh* remarked on how the road between Leith and Musselburgh had to retreat inland the road has had to be removed again and again. Many are the tracts of golf links which have disappeared. The great stretch of sand in Aberlady Bay, certainly represents a movement in the other direction, but such extensions of the land along the Lothian coast are due not to little rivers such as the Mill Burn, but to the build-up of eroded sand and stones by the movements of the tides. All along this shore raised beaches can be detected. The hundred-foot beach is well marked near Gullane.

West of Aberlady Bay again is the great sweep of Gosford Bay. Seawards, the view is breathtaking, especially on a still evening, when the crags and castle and spires of Edinburgh are painted on the sunset with the diaphanous brushwork of a Turner. Landwards, there is nothing to be seen but a massive stone wall which hugs the inner side of the road backed by a dense hedge of trees, whose tops, bent by the salt winds, thrust backwards in a nearly impenetrable barrier. In the park behind this barrier lies Gosford House, seat of the Earls of Wemyss and March, a very striking essay in classicism, set among formal gardens. The estate formerly seems to have been a stretch of open links, and an eighteenth-century Lord Wemyss made a practice of coming over from Amisfield to golf there. Eventually he bought the land. There was only a small house, and so he commissioned Robert Adam to draw up plans for an appropriate residence, but first Adam and then his patron died, then the next earl dismantled some of the work which had been done. His successor, in spite of the fortune which had been spent, would have liked to pull the whole thing down. Not until 1870 was it decided to complete this extraordinary building, and an unknown architect called Young —later to build the Municipal Buildings in Glasgow—was given the task. Despite the lapse in time, it is a very fine realisation of an Adam concept.

South-west of Gosford Bay lies a string of coastal villages : Port Seton, Cockenzie and Prestonpans. This over-urgent age by-passes them neatly, for the main coast road doubles back to Longniddry and goes on its way to Edinburgh at a safe distance inland. It leaves the three villages like an enclave of the past, the not-so-distant past as anyone looking at the straggling houses can see, but nevertheless a past unlikely to come round again. Here and there what is left is of real beauty, as for example Northfield House at Prestonpans. This lovely seventeenth-century mansion set in a gracious garden was built by an Edinburgh merchant of the name of Marjoribanks. Another mansion of about the same time is Preston House, built for the son of an Edinburgh Lord Provost, a building now largely in ruins ; and there is Preston Tower, a stronghold of a century or two earlier, destroyed by Cromwell in 1650 for its owners' Covenanting persuasion. But the villages themselves have not the air or the patina of age of those older buildings, if they have still a good deal of the picturesque. Their interest lies rather in being the crumbling shells of vanished industries and ways of life. They are now not much more than the litter of a past prosperity along the shore, and in some lights the windows of the houses seem to look with something like dumb incomprehension at the Firth which not so long ago yielded the harvests which built them.

Two hundred and fifty years ago the combined trade of those three villages was comparable to the trade of Leith, the port of Edinburgh. It is not so long since the brown sails of the fishing fleets were seen in Cockenzie and Port Seton harbours. Certainly when I was a boy it was still possible to buy here on Edinburgh's doorstep kippers of a flavour and fatness now unobtainable. Recently I stood on the deserted front here and looked across the Firth at the smoke of Kirkcaldy on the opposite shore, reflecting how that dimly-seen town had produced in Adam Smith a man whose thoughts had been turned by smaller men into that science of economics which decrees that it is better to export for profit kippers which our grandfathers would not have deigned to taste than to profit from the enjoyment of properly cured kippers as God meant us to do. Up to a century ago the fishermen from those two villages went in their open, deckless boats to even the distant fishing-grounds, and between times got whitefish in the Firth or dredged oysters in the beds offshore. There was whale-fishing from Cockenzie, too, as there are more jawbones than the ones on North Berwick Law to testify, even now, and one expedition at least found itself marooned for a polar winter in Baffin Bay. A fine new harbour and breakwater were built at Cockenzie as lately as 1880, but Cockenzie, like most of the other ports on both shores of the Firth, was doomed. I do not think there is any trace left in Prestonpans of the high walls of the vitriol factory which Faujas St. Fond found here in 1784, describing it as the greatest of its kind in Britain. It was founded in 1749 by the Dr. John Roebuck who was to do so much for the Scottish iron industry a few years later. Indeed, the friend who steered Roebuck's thoughts towards Scottish ore was William Cadell, the ship-owner and importer of neighbouring Cockenzie. At an early date both Cockenzie and Port Seton, for some reason, boasted machines for grinding natural fertilisers and for expressing oil from linseed, the residue being made into cattlecake, employments which the *Statistical Account* says "do not seem prejudicial either to health or morals." The parish's principal manufacture, however, used to be salt, the iron pans for evaporating which attached the suffix "pans" to the original name of Preston. This industry was founded by an Earl of Winton in 1630, although the monks of Newbattle were believed to have established salt-making here five centuries earlier. Before the end of the eighteenth century there was a production of more than 80,000 bushels and Prestonpans could supply all the east of Scotland ; but the repeal of the salt duty in 1825 spelt the end of this, and soon the pans were rusting and the girnels empty and left to fall down.

The medieval monks of Newbattle found more than salt at Prestonpans. The monks were assiduous investigators and cultivators of all natural resources, and in this locality their spades turned up a clay of more than usually excellent quality, which they proceeded to turn into bricks and into those tiles embossed with animals which were dug up in the nunnery at North Berwick and are now to be seen in the National Museum of Antiquities. When the monks departed the clay beds were not forgotten. There is no evidence that the merchants dealing with the Low Countries were interested in them, but on the other hand it is believed that the potters of Delft received a good deal of coal from the Lothians, probably through Prestonpans and its neighbouring ports. However, the real development of the Prestonpans potteries dates from the middle of the eighteenth century, when more than 70 potters were employed in two potteries. The date might even be placed a good deal earlier, for there were potters in the village fifty years before, and nearly fifty years before that there is a record of glass being made from the sand and kelp on the shore, heated in crucibles made from a local pipe-clay. But by 1755 Prestonpans was of sufficient repute to attract four English craftsmen who were not only potters but skilled in making porcelain, and before they came the Scots seem already to have been producing some kind of whiteware. There were two main factories. George Gordon's, which lay somewhere in the Bankfoot end of the place, was the better known. The blue-and-white printed wares are as beautiful as anything of their kind being made at the time, but Gordon must have turned out thousands of teapots and jugs and figure groups decorated in rather violent, " cottagey " colours. He also made basalt wares such as Wedgwood made, from a local clay got at Upper Birslie out of pits which were known long after as the Clayholes. The rival pottery was Watson's, sited on the shore a little west of the church. The village folk called it the Pott-Works, and it is said to have had a turnover of £5,000 in its first year. Its main output seems to have been figures, and its English potters shaped these in their own, southern way, using local types such as fishwives, or kilted men. Decorated Prestonpans punchbowls were at one time common in the Lothians, as the practice was to give one, perhaps with his name inscribed, to the incoming tenant of a farm. At a humbler level, Watson's made salt-glazed stoneware bottles for the celebrated tuppeny ale of Prestonpans, and when at last the company failed it was taken over by the brewers, John Fowler & Co. Red clay inkwells were another mass product of this factory and in the days of the dominies they were to be found in village schools all over Scotland. The potters of Prestonpans may have had no poets like the weavers of Paisley had, but like them they were thrifty and could boast what to-day is called solidarity. The Potters' Friendly Society had a thousand members, and the first Friday in June down to the year 1840, was Potters' Day when there was a procession and much jollity. A skilled potter such as a figure maker could earn as much as 15s. per week; but the secret of the excellence of Prestonpans pottery lies in the mastery of the craftsmen over all processes from throwing to firing, so that they took a pride in the finished article as no mere specialist in the over-organised trades of to-day is likely to do.

Occasionally one comes on Prestonpans pots or jugs showing a rather garish trooper leaping his horse over a cannon. This, of course, commemorates the battle of Prestonpans. The battlefield is in fact nearer Preston. Sir John Cope and the Government troops were drawn up facing east behind the road joining Cockenzie and Tranent, a high wall at their backs and a ditch and bog on their right flank. Prince Charles Edward had come out from Edinburgh to meet them, swinging round to face them from high ground before dusk on 20th September, 1745. The books tend to stress for obvious reasons the inequality of a fight between Cope's trained troops and the Prince's wild Highlandmen, and even Hume Brown, who admits to a fair balance of strength, implies an armament of scythes and suchlike weapons on the rebels' side; but given the right circumstances the clansman's tactics were difficult to counter, as Killiecrankie had shown. Under cover of the dark the Prince led his men by a secret path across the bog and, screened by one of those early-morning autumnal sea-mists, drew up his order of battle under Cope's nose. Cope was a slow-witted, conventional soldier —" Hey Johnnie Cope, are ye wauken yet ? "—and had taken no precautions to forestall such a move. The Highlanders made their usual pattern of attack. They discharged their pistols, threw them away, and with targe on left arm and broadsword flashing fell on their enemies, taking the bayonet points on the tough wooden, leather-covered shields while they butchered the momentarily disarmed infantry. The bayonets remained blood-less, as someone noticed afterwards. In just ten minutes panic seized Cope's men. They tried to fly, but many were brought up against the wall behind. Only Colonel Gardiner remained to attempt to rally them, but he was cut down on the field within sight of his own house of Bankton. Where he was buried is not known, but there is a tall memorial to him in the park of Bankton House carrying a verse by Hugh Miller. His sword, a fine basket-hilted blade, now belongs to the Murray-Thriepland family and for many years has been on loan to the Royal Scottish Museum.

The country around Prestonpans is now the meeting-place of the arable farmlands of East Lothian and the great market-gardening area just east of Edinburgh. The bog through which Prince Charlie led his army is one of many which have been reclaimed and turned into holdings of astonishing productivity. The raised beach which we came across at Gullane continues all along this coast, and for a spade deep or more there is a fine light loam lying on a subsoil of gravel and shell, a well-drained tilth which warms up long before the clammy clays and benefits by the low rainfall and comparatively good sunshine records of this corner of the country. Even as early as the day of the *Statistical Account* there is reference to these " mail-gardens," as they seem to have been called, supplying the Edinburgh and Glasgow markets with fresh vegetables, and one tenant of that time (1845) is cited as paying as much as £100 a year in rent for his garden. In spring and early summer, when leeks and greens are small or crops still under lines of flashing cloches, the villadom of the capital's suburbs is varied with great areas which look like some view of Hillegom or the borders of the Wash, but for the contours of the ground. The total area under market-garden cultivation from Aberlady to Musselburgh is something like 4000 acres and it produces well over half the vegetables grown in Scotland. The tradition of market-gardening hereabouts may go back as far as the Middle Ages, and many of the families now in the industry have inherited their skills through many generations. A considerable body of labour is necessary, 3 acres per worker being the estimated requirement, and at planting and harvesting the numbers of course increase greatly. With so long a period of intensive cultivation the soil is exceptionally fertile. Indeed, in some places soil dug from these gardens has been described as an excellent sample of manure! At one time the building up of a rich, organic soil was no great problem, as natural manure could be bought from the nearby city in huge quantities, and no doubt the prosperity of the Lothian market gardener to-day can to a considerable extent be traced to the fortunate history of his land. The gardener now keeps little stock, if indeed any at all. The city's numerous stables have become garages, with no profitable by-products, but fortunately some of its sewage is now being "farmed" to produce that pungently antiseptic-smelling grey ooze which they tell me is excellent plant-food. Few of the gardeners depend on "artificials" alone, or the priceless capital of the fertility of their land would rapidly disappear. Much compost and green manure is used. The larger of the gardens range between 100 and 200 acres, and they grow salad crops, together with leeks, peas, beetroot and rhubarb, while the small places specialise in early vegetables and, under glass, grow tomatoes to be followed by chrysanthemums after the crop is taken. A slight north slope discourages too early sprouting, so that as a rule there is a minimum of frost damage, and it may be that this has contributed much to the success of the Musselburgh leek-growers, whose plants seem to be so much less prone to "shoot" than are those from other areas. It is believed that this famous strain of leek is a cross between a plant imported from the Low Countries and a local seashore plant with the name *Allium ampeloprasum*. At Stoneyhill there is one of the biggest "French" market-gardens in Britain, and here the widespread use of glass and of heating-pipes under the soil have forced production up to seven crops a year.

In Musselburgh the arbitrary coastal strip which I have called the Lower Frith ends with an overlap from East Lothian into Midlothian. Musselburgh is a long, straggling town which straddles the mouth of the Esk. Like other little Lothian streams, the Esk can become a dangerous flood at times, but normally it murmurs, brown and shallow, between grassy banks. The town itself is perhaps not as impressive as its ancient right to the title of Royal Burgh might suggest, but the central section of it, where the street is generously planned, with here and there characterful old buildings and, at one end, glimpses of some great old trees, makes up for the less-distinguished environs. The most memorable building is the tolbooth, or town house, well placed at a corner where the main street widens. It was rebuilt in 1590, after being destroyed in Hertford's invasion, like so much else in the Lothians, but the council chamber with its corbelled parapet walk was added in the eighteenth century, with its peculiarly pleasing angled forestair. The building still houses the municipal offices, and a marble panel inside the porch carries the inscription : " Magistrates do Justice in the fear of God, June 16th, 1773." With the inscription is the burgh arms of three mussel shells within three anchors. The tolbooth steeple itself, notably its roof, is quite clearly Dutch in inspiration like so many other buildings along the shores of the Firth, and the original clock is said to have been a gift from the Dutch, with whom there were close trade relations. The name is taken from the big beds of mussels lying off the mouth of the Esk. The ancient boast of the town that it was a burgh before Edinburgh achieved that status is not impossible, for the grant dates from the reign of David I : the capital city's can be traced no further than this.

Musselburgh is more conscious of its past glories than are most burghs in Scotland. Perhaps proximity to Edinburgh has something to do with this. The Riding of the Marches takes place less often than in the Border towns, but when it does there is a Town Champion in shining armour and a great deal of accompanying ceremonial which includes the digging of " divots " of turf at the town boundaries. On Musselburgh Links there is a racecourse where the " Edinburgh " Races take place twice a year, and have done since 1816 ; but a more ancient if less popular occasion on the same Links is the annual visit of

Lennoxlove was for 300 years the home of the Maitlands. The tower dates from the fifteenth century

the Royal Company of Archers, the Queen's Bodyguard for Scotland, who in their magnificent uniforms shoot for the Musselburgh Silver Arrow. In the old days the victor received £1.10s. from the town, and a " riddel full " (that is, one dozen) of claret, while he had to attach to the Arrow a gold or silver medal recording his feat. The Arrow is kept with others of its kind at Archers' Hall in Edinburgh. At the east end of the High Street is the entrance to the grounds of Loretto School, one of the few public schools on English lines in Scotland. The name derives from the old convent of Our Lady of Loretto, which has now almost totally disappeared. First destroyed in the Hertford invasion, the exposure of a fraudulent miracle concerning the " cure " of a blind man hastened its dissolution just prior to the Reformation ; but if we are to believe Sir David Lyndsay of the Mount the Hermitage of Loretto got itself a rather dubious reputation :

> I have sene pass ane marvellous multitude,
> Young men and women flingand on thair feit,
> Under the forme of feinzeit sanctitude,
> For till adore ane image in Laureit (Loretto) ;
> Mony came with thair marrowis for to meit.

The intercessionary powers of the Hermitage seem to have been connected especially with marriage and birth, and James V is believed to have made a pilgrimage to it on foot all the way from Stirling in 1536 before setting out on his marriage venture to France. The sequel, it may be remembered, was such a degree of disillusionment on meeting his bride-to-be, Marie de Vendôme —" bossue et contrfaicte," he found her !—that the match was broken off ; but he went on to marry Madeleine, daughter of the French king, in great state at Notre Dame and returned with her and a splendid following, including the poet Ronsard, so that his pilgrimage to Loretto did not go unrewarded. When the Hermitage was destroyed the ruins were used as a quarry for the building of the tolbooth in the town, for which piece of sacrilege the Pope laid an annual curse on the men of Mussel-burgh until about a century and a half ago. But if Loretto School to-day cannot point to the Hermitage from which it got its name it now possesses the fine Renaissance building of Pinkie House,

The Bass Rock seen from the ruins of Tantallon Castle

erected in 1613 by Alexander, Lord Seton, "not as he would have wished," as an inscription has it, "but according to the measure of his means and estate." It is a curious but impressive blend of the vernacular tradition with English features such as the big oriel window, and there is in the courtyard a superb Renaissance well-head surmounted by an open crown in the style of the steeple of St. Giles' in Edinburgh. The crowning glory of Pinkie House, however, is its Painted Gallery. 78 feet long, this gallery has a timber ceiling, coved at the sides, on which *in tempera* some artist, possibly an Italian, has tried to represent a barrel vault and a lantern. The perspective treatment is skilful, but the illusion created is much less important than the general splendour of the effect.

The district of the burgh to the west of the mouth of the Esk is Fisherrow. Fisherrow's identity has been, until quite recently at least, quite distinct from Musselburgh's, for the fishing community which lived there was self-contained, had its own traditions and way of life, like the even more celebrated community at Newhaven a few miles west, which still fosters its own traditions. Fisherrow never seems to have been a very great fishing-port—there were only seven boats as far back as 1793—but the smacks came in here from all along the Fife coast and landed their fish for the Edinburgh market. On this there flourished the profession of the fishwives. The number of boats fishing from Fisherrow increased greatly in the nineteenth century, but throughout its history it is the fishwives who have made the community distinctive. They had of course their picturesque costume, as the Newhaven fishwives have to-day, and they travelled long distances to dispose of the catches, carrying on their backs their great osier creels. If the boats came in late, the catches would be speeded to Edinburgh by relay deliveries and the five miles to the market done in three-quarters of an hour. There is a case on record of three of these fishwives each carrying a heavy load of herrings from Dunbar to Edinburgh, a distance of twenty-seven miles, in five hours! The fishwives have always been bred to their job from infancy, and intermarriage was the rule.

Although the fishing has passed, Musselburgh has never endangered her prosperity by putting all her eggs in one basket.

There have been mills of various sorts, a broadcloth factory, breweries, soapworks, potteries, tanworks. None of them has lasted as long as the market-gardening industry already described which first came into being under the direction of the monks of Newbattle. The knitting of fishing-nets was practised, but some time after the Napoleonic war a Musselburgh man of the name of James Paterson invented and patented a loom for weaving the nets, starting a factory in 1820 which had increased to eighteen looms by 1839. In 1850 the business was taken over by an Edinburgh firm, which at once expanded it, so that to-day it is one of the greatest fishing-net factories in the world. Another well-established Musselburgh industry which has expanded to meet new needs is wire and wire-rope making. This big firm, its humming shops controlling all processes from the rolling of the steel billets to the weaving of the ropes from the resulting wire, was the first to produce stainless steel wire ropes on a commercial scale, the first to draw nickel alloy steel into wire, and the first to make high-grade streamline wires and tie-rods for the aircraft industry. Its research department has originated many invaluable things from lubricating greases to stress-testing machines. The Esk, rippling under its bridges, may be a modest river, but on its banks, whether in Musselburgh or further up, as we shall see in the chapter which follows, prosperity is usually not far to seek.

CHAPTER FOUR

Black Soil

ONE OF the bridges across the Esk at Musselburgh, a handsome triple-spanned structure with, certainly, a hoary appearance, used to be attributed to the Romans. This belief was perpetuated even by the compilers of the *Statistical Account*. The bridge in fact dates from the sixteenth century, maybe erected by the widow of the Lord Seton who fell at Flodden. The Romans, however, were firmly established about the mouth of the Esk and on the heights overlooking it. Not so long ago in his excavations the gravedigger used to throw up fragments of Samian ware and other pottery used in the Roman colonies in the first and second centuries, and there have been coins of several emperors, including Hadrian, to say nothing of the more substantial remains which I will mention presently. Here the highway from the south which crossed the Lammermuirs at Soutra came down to the sea, and here we may be sure the galleys brought in heavy material to supply the legions. Chalmers in his *Caledonia* hints at a seafront on which the officers of the Roman garrison had built themselves pleasant villas to remind them in their exile of the delights of the Bay of Baiæ and the "Volscian strand." By the time Scotland felt the tread of the legions it is certain that the legionaries and their officers were a mixed lot and had probably never known Baiæ, but enough remains in this neighbourhood to show they had learned how to make themselves comfortable in the Roman way.

Evidence of the Roman occupation was obvious enough to attract attention even amid the turbulence of the sixteenth century. An altar was discovered—"a Monument of Grit Antiquitie "—in the spring of 1565, and in spite of her many pre-occupations Queen Mary herself charged the bailies of Musselburgh that it " be nocht demolisit nor broken down." A Roman bath was disclosed at the same time. Just what the Scots

made of their discovery at this time we do not know; but
Randolph, the observant ambassador of Queen Elizabeth, a few
days after the monument's appearance, writes to Sir William
Cecil that "The cave found bysyds Muskelbourge seemeth to
be some monument of the Romaynes, by a stone that was found,
with these words greven upon hym. 'Appolini Granno Q. L.
Sabiniaunus Proc. Aug.' (and) Dyvers short pillars sette upright
upon the grounde covered with tyle stones, large and thyucke,
torning into dyvers angles and certayne places lyke unto chynes
to awoid smoke. Thys is all that I can gather thereof." The
great Napier of Merchiston describes the altar in 1593. It was
seen again in Inveresk kirkyard about 1700, with the lettering
almost weathered away, but now it is gone. Apollo Grannus
was one of the strange gods of the northern frontiers of the
Roman empire, a Celtic god of healing merged in the Apollo
concept.

Subsequent disclosures have shown that the main Roman
settlement was not by the sea, but on the ridge or high ground
inland where the village of Inveresk now is. Not much of this
settlement remains either : only some foundations and a corner
of a hypocaust in the grounds of Inveresk House. The hypocaust
consists of a few stubby stone pillars, such as Randolph describes,
supporting a rough slab. The poverty of evidence about the
settlement, however, is due to local indifference, for in 1783
some gardeners working east of the church came upon the remains
of the foundations and floors of whole groups of buildings.
They exposed a space 60 feet long by 23 feet broad intersected by
a network of walls and chambers, apparently including baths
complete with hypocaust, beside which was a supply of charcoal
for the furnace. The clay flues for conducting the heat were
quite perfect. Not only this, but all around were fragments of
other buildings. The concrete or mortar used is said to have been
of as fine a quality as that used to line the sewers of Rome itself,
and the bricks of good workmanship although the river pebbles
they contained no doubt came from the bed of the Esk. Everything points to an important Roman post at Inveresk. It may
well have extended along the entire length of the ridge as far as
Pinkie Burn, for the story goes that towards the end of the
eighteenth century there were so many ancient pavements here-

abouts that it was difficult to use a horse and plough. There were remains too of a camp on the low ground south-west of the village, with a causeway linking it to the settlement at Fisherrow. Whilst Roman outposts remained north of the Forth, the colonists of Inveresk must have lived a peaceful and even comfortable life, their well-warmed homes defying even the insidious east-coast haars ; but at the end of the second century Clodius Albinus withdrew not only outposts but garrisons in his effort to win for himself the Purple, and at once the tide of the Picts flowed hungrily southwards, far beyond the Border, destroying not only the forts but no doubt also the villas and baths and all other amenities of the intruders.

The old kirk of St. Michael in Inveresk, visible on its ridge for miles around, is supposed to have been built in part with material quarried from the Roman township, but the existing kirk is a replacement of the early nineteenth century. There is still an old building or two, however. Both Inveresk Lodge and Halkerston are good, simple examples of late-seventeenth century Scots domestic architecture. The first is not to be confused with Inveresk House, in the garden of which is the Roman hypocaust : this was built in 1597 by the parish minister, Adam Colt. Another parish minister brought fame, if not indeed notoriety, to the village. This was Alexander Carlyle, better known perhaps as " Jupiter " Carlyle, who was a leading example of the Moderate movement which captured the Kirk in the middle of the eighteenth century. The Moderates preferred to temper the zeal of evangelical tradition and saw no reason why they should turn their backs on good living, nor why they should limit their scholarship to the requirements of theological discussion. Carlyle was something of an extremist in this movement. He went so far as to write satirically about those who frowned on playing cards on Sundays, and he was among the small group of ministers who in 1756 went to the theatre to see the production of *Douglas* by the Rev. John Home, drawing from the Presbytery of Edinburgh the memorable injunction that " all within its bounds discourage the illegal and dangerous entertainments of the stage, and restrain those under their influence from frequenting such seminaries of vice and folly." Carlyle stoutly continued to patronise the theatre and was an admirer of Mrs. Siddons.

The manse of Inveresk became a resort of the lions of Edinburgh's golden age. Robertson the historian came here, Dugald Stewart and Tobias Smollett, and even the archsceptic David Hume, whilst a good part of *Douglas* is thought to have been written in the house, to say nothing of Carlyle's own celebrated *Autobiography*. In the *Statistical Account* Carlyle is not listed among the "Eminent Men" of the parish, although the list includes the name of David Macbeth Moir, the literary doctor of Inveresk, yet to-day we should probably agree that the *Autobiography* will wear better than *Mansie Wauch*.

The rich soil of this corner of Midlothian has produced not only superb vegetables but lovely gardens and beauty spots. As in most other places, the gardens and the beauty spots are less numerous than they were. Around Carberry Tower, however, a mile or two from Inveresk, is some of the finest landscape gardening in Scotland : not in the semi-wild, grand manner of Inverewe, with it adventitious aids of sea and mountain, but in a more English style of lawns and water-vistas dappled with floating lilies and overhung by willows. In the cultivation of exotics, a challenge which so many northern gardeners feel they must take up, the east coast cannot of course compete with the west, where the mild sea air keeps frosts at bay, but Carberry has its sheltered nooks where foreign plants have been induced to flourish, and Californian visitors will be delighted by a noble avenue of Sequoias, now not so far from being a century old. Glimpsed through the glades is Carberry Tower itself, an ivy-covered mansion. The original portion, the tower, dates from the first half of the sixteenth century, and the first of the subsequent additions was built in the 1590s. The earliest owner seems to have been Hew Rigg, an advocate. Knox in his *History* relates that it was said Rigg and the Abbot of Dunfermline between them were responsible for the Scots army leaving its strong position above the Esk in the battle of Pinkie in 1547, inviting disaster exactly as happened at the battle of Dunbar a few miles further east a century later. Rigg's motive is believed to have been to save Carberry from destruction. "Men of judgment liked not the journey," says Knox, "for they thought it no wisdom to leave their strength." And so it certainly proved, for the Scots down in Pinkie Cleuch came under the double fire of Somerset's army on Fawside Hill and of the English ships in the mouth of the Esk, and a disastrous rout followed which ended only next day with the putting of Leith to the flames. The English motive, however, of breaking the Franco-Scottish alliance and achieving a marriage between the little Mary Queen of Scots and Edward VI, was not accomplished. In the early nineteenth century the soil by Pinkie Burn was found to be full of the bones of horses slaughtered in the How Mire by the English fire of three hundred years before, when the waters of the burn are said to have run red for three days. It was on Carberry Hill near here, too, twenty years later, that Mary watched Bothwell, her husband of a month, go from her for the last time to pursue the piracy that brought him to his end, while she gave herself up to the Confederate Lords and began the journey to Lochleven.

Above Inveresk there are two or three winding miles of river, with heavy-yielding fields on either bank. Then comes the confluence of the South and the North Esks, the first coming down from the Lammermuirs, the second from the Pentland Hills away to the west. A mile up the North Esk, in a spacious park, stands Dalkeith Palace. It is built on a great outcrop of rock, with lawns below stretching to the river's edge, dark drifts of rhododendron and darker-shadowed woods and copses. In the main, the Palace is a characteristic piece of Scottish neo-classicism of the early eighteenth century, with an eastern frontage of nearly 150 feet centred not on a portico but on four Corinthian pilasters carrying entablature and pediment, and clusters of those tall chimneys which, in an English building of the kind, would probably have been hid. It was built by Vanbrugh for Anne, Duchess of Buccleuch and Monmouth, and modelled on the larger Palace of Loo in Holland. Much of the stone used came from an earlier structure on the spot, and portions of the fifteenth-century castle are in the rear incorporated in the Palace. The magnificence of the interior matches the stately views of park and woods and river. One great, finely-proportioned chamber leads to another, with marble floors and fireplaces, superb oak panelling, and a grand staircase with a gilt iron balustrade of great beauty. The collection of paintings has few rivals in other Scottish country mansions. When a westering

sun fills the dining-room it lights Kneller's portrait of the original
owner with her sons ; but several of the greatest masters of
Renaissance Italy and of the Low Countries are represented by
works. When Duchess Anne married Monmouth, Charles II
presented his son with furniture which is still in the Palace. This
is a palace in concept as well as in name, and it is scarcely surprising to know that Queen Victoria and her Consort made a stay
there, like George IV before her.

Other kings and men of eminence in history spent time in
the castle whose remnants are knit with the Palace. Froissart
seems to have visited the place about 1360 and seen the original
castle captured by Edward III twenty years earlier. This was in
the possession of the Douglases, who had Dalkeith for another
three centuries at the cost of an annual gift to the King of a pair
of white gloves or a silver penny at the Feast of Pentecost. In
1519, when the plague was in Edinburgh, the court of James V
moved to the castle of Dalkeith for a time. James VI came for a
day a hundred years later, and Charles I slept there for a night
in 1633. It was nine years later that it passed to the Buccleuchs.
Not all its royal occasions together seem to have matched the
grandeur of Duchess Anne's early days in her new-built Palace,
for she kept sovereign state, allowing no one to sit in her presence,
even at dinner, when a canopy was held over her and pages
ministered to her wants.

Dalkeith town, together with Eskbank, is the main nodal
point near Edinburgh of north-south with east-west traffic.
Neither is in itself distinguished, but both are prosperous
accumulations of shops and villas with a few Victorian steeples
rising from among the huddles of blue-grey roofs. Only one of
the kirks is of a respectable age : the West Parish Church, once
called the Collegiate Church of St. Nicholas ; but a good deal
of this is reconstructed, and the choir is without a roof. Cromwell, with his usual fine disregard for other people's religious
feelings, stabled his horses in it. Of former ornaments, little
remains ; but there is a pair of effigies not so time-worn that their
dignity and beauty have quite gone, and enough detail is preserved on their shields of arms to suggest they are monuments to
James Douglas, first Earl of Morton, and his wife Joanna,
daughter of James I.

Even now, when many who live in Dalkeith and Eskbank go to work in Edinburgh, the two small towns are no satellites of the city whose smoke drifts towards them on a north wind. The past prosperity of Dalkeith was soundly based on the fine farming lands around it. It has been famous as a market-town since the Middle Ages, and was Scotland's greatest market for her staple grain of oats, a year's sales a hundred years ago amounting to 43,000 quarters and nearly 7000 bags of oatmeal. On market-day the carts came rumbling in from an early hour from all the south-eastern counties of Scotland, piled high with produce, and sometimes, totalling many hundreds, they filled the length of the High Street on both sides. At noon the church bell announced the opening of the grain market, and half an hour later its clanging signified the start of the wheat sales. The most notable feature of the event, however, was that all dealing was in ready money, and completed at high speed, the whole of the proceedings being ended in a maximum time of two hours, conducted apparently with the utmost animation and good will. Well supplied with all the simple needs, Dalkeith grew to be the healthiest of communities, and clearly there was more than its " pine-scented air " to attract the numerous invalids who used to come from Edinburgh. The scent of pines is no longer one of the more noticeable amenities, but happily the town still possesses big flour mills which know how to grind wheat as it should be ground, and do so. The people of Dalkeith are by tradition practical, and of all the stories of the town's worthies I like best the account of Dr. Porteous, who went over to the Church of England and left a sum of money to the village of Hunton, in Kent, the interest to be divided among the six parishioners who were the most regular churchgoers. Porteous became a Bishop of London.

Between Dalkeith and Edinburgh the countryside borrows most of its attraction from the distant views. It cannot always have been so : there were great remnants of the ancient forest where royal huntsmen gave chase to deer of exceptional size, and there are still stretches of fine woodland around such places as Melville Castle or The Drum. Yet the boundary of the city has reached out southwards, taking in more and more of the broad fields, bringing a plague of prosaic housing to meadows where knights once jousted or poets walked in contemplation. Craigmillar Castle, the principal historic monument in this area, is now within the city limits and therefore belongs with the city rather than with the county region which concerns us now ; but as a favourite resort of Mary Queen of Scots it made its influence felt for some distance around. The castle, even in its present ruinous state, dominates from its hill the country about it. Its massive fourteenth-century L-shaped tower itself dominates the extensive outworks that the builders of the fifteenth and sixteenth centuries heaped against it. The great angle towers and their curtain walls have outlasted the burning by Hertford in 1544. Mary's attachment to Craigmillar can be read even on the destination-signs of some of the buses passing within sight of the castle, which advertise they are on their way to Little France, a hamlet a short distance along the Dalkeith road where Mary's French servants are believed to have had their lodgings. Similarly, Burdiehouse, a mile or two away, Scots-sounding though it be, is thought to have got its name from the queen's French followers, who called it Bordeaux House. Incidentally, near Burdiehouse there is a reminder of the immense riches which underlie this part of the Lothians. In the grounds of St. Catherine's there is a very old well known as the Balm Well, the black, scummy water of which was prized in the middle ages for its power to cure skin complaints. Boece tells of it in 1526. The legend has it that the oil of St. Catherine was being brought from Mount Sinai for Queen Margaret, when some drops of it were spilt. The surface oil rises, in fact, from the shale beds of Straiton. It may have been found beneficial by the leper colony which gave its name to Liberton nearby.

On the opposite side of Dalkeith and Eskbank is the vale of Newbattle. It is no longer the secluded, romantic spot that Scott found it, but the mansion of Newbattle remains one of the most interesting houses in this part of the country. Properly still called Newbattle Abbey, the house has been built in comparatively recent times on the foundations of the ancient abbey which exerted such influence on the development of the county, and the plan of the abbey is marked out on the lawns by means of gravel and by inlaid pieces on the floors of various rooms in the house. It must have been one of the choicest as well as one of the richest Cistercian foundations in Scotland, an offshoot of Melrose created by David I in 1140, lying on a meadow bordered by the South Esk. How rich the abbey was may be judged by the quality of fragments of stone carving which have survived, especially the portion of a St. Barbara which by its costume can be dated somewhere in the fifteenth century and also a fine sixteenth-century font. It has been estimated that about the time the St. Barbara was carved the abbey had income enough to maintain eighty monks and almost as many lay brethren, and the plan which has been reconstructed after many years of excavations shows an important establishment, with an aisled church 240 feet long shadowing a square cloister surrounded by chapter house, library, vestry, frater and all the usual offices. The destruction of the abbey, as of most of the other sacred houses in the south of Scotland, happened during the Hertford invasion of 1544. The Reformation did not obliterate it finally, as one might expect. As late as 1597 six very old monks were still living and going about their devotions in the cloisters, and the fire-blackened stones had been painfully gathered together to set up another church, in the vault of which the last abbot, Mark Kerr, was buried. Kerr was in minor orders only. He married, and his son was created Baron Newbottle—Newbottle being the old, and the correct rendering of the name. To this title others were added, until in 1701 a descendant of Kerr became the first Marquis of Lothian.

The house of Lothian had its home at the Abbey for more than three centuries. Few families could show a more consistent record of public service, and its members were staunch fighters for the Protestant cause, either as Covenanters in the field or as Commissioners in the Assembly. The Lothians accumulated a tradition of scholarship, too, and the family's cultural attainments—there is a window to the memory of the eighth marquis in Christchurch, Oxford—brought a new distinction to the old Abbey, and with it works of art and treasures of many kinds. Its library gathered a number of rare manuscripts and early books. On its walls, Vandyke was added to Vandyke, among them the famous triple head of Charles I given by the king to Strafford before his execution, and Rembrandt to Dürer, together with painted chests, church vestments and a great variety of antiquities. At last the Abbey, with many of its contents, was left by the marquis who, until the Second World War, was British Ambassador in Washington, to be devoted to adult education. It is now a residential college, with a small number of students pursuing short courses of philosophy, it may be, or economics or literature, fortunate in an atmosphere of scholarship and accomplishment. Behind, fine forest trees screen the Abbey from the clamour of industrialism, and soft carpets of turf add to the air of seclusion.

The deep loam of the vale must once have nourished a very snug little community, but scarcely anything is left of the old village which lay at the Abbey gates. There are an early eighteenth century church and inn and a manse which may be a hundred years older. One minister of this little, vanished village, the Rev. Andrew Cant, a zealous Covenanter, had a repute which has survived the attempt to make his name the origin of the word for ranting hypocrisy. A more credible claim is that he was connected with Immanuel Kant. Kant's grandfather was certainly a Scot and is believed to have come from the north country, where Andrew Cant originated and whither he returned to be the stubborn opponent of the episcopalianism to which Aberdeen clung. By a nice piece of irony, his successor as minister of Newbattle was Robert Leighton, who was destined to forsake Presbytery and go over to Episcopacy, becoming eventually Archbishop of Glasgow. Leighton was no zealot. A saintly man, he spent his life trying to reconcile the form of worship which he adopted with the one he had abandoned, but he succeeded only in being misliked by the adherents of both in that time of fanaticism.

From Newbattle, it is impossible to move further in any direction without being confronted with the greatest industrial issue in the Lothians—coal. In the wooded dells of these parts it may be possible to escape the signs of it for a little while ; but close around Newbattle is descending the clutter of immense new developments, and even the once-lonely Camp Hill on whose summit are the ramparts of an ancient fort is being encroached upon by a new community which alone will number something like 20,000. In Newtongrange the road narrows between structures which are the very core of the great industry, and the upperworks of the Lingerwood and Lady Victoria pits at the south end of the town represent a growing prosperity which stretches over—or under—the heart of the Lothians.

The coal measures run deep here. The shafts of those pits are among the deepest in the country. I have a sharp recollection of the Lady Victoria, where many years ago I had my first experience of the depths of a coal mine. Its galleries run for great distances from the pit-bottom. It is difficult in the wan light of those endless galleries, still more crouched under a low, raw, glinting ceiling at the pit-face, with the occasional unearthly creak of the rock-mass which the miners speak of familiarly as the pit " talking," to imagine the pretty streams and woods half a mile above one's head. Awesome as all this seems to a new-comer, the conditions in this coalfield are in fact the best in Scotland, partly because there is comparatively little faulting in the coal measures. The strata rear up suddenly around Camp Hill presenting what is called Edge Coal, and the problem in this area is to work away from the small area of workable coal in the vertical seams by driving horizontal galleries to connect with distant seams. The coal-bearing strata dip away again towards the East Lothian basin, and then to the north dip under the Firth itself to come up again in Fife.

This uprearing of the seams to the surface in the vicinity of Newbattle seems to have had the attention of the monks at the abbey as early as the thirteenth century. They set men to work collecting the " black stanis " which gave off " sik intolerable heit " no doubt at first in surface mines which gradually became shallow pits, but development was slow in days when men could get all the warmth they wanted for ordinary purposes from wood and peat, and it was 1526 before the monks built a harbour to ship the coal away by sea. Moreover, as the heughs had to be worked deeper to follow the coal down the miner's job became a more and more unpleasant one, attended by greater and greater dangers, so that by 1606 the Scots Parliament had to pass an Act tying the miners to their jobs in such a way that if they left they could be prosecuted for, in effect, stealing themselves ! Even by the time of the invasion by Somerset in 1547 the mining community was extensive and the underground workings in the Tranent area alone so numerous that the whole village hid itself in them, only to be suffocated or driven out when the invaders blocked up the exits and lit fires in them. The use of coal was spreading everywhere. It became so profitable to send it away in ships in ballast that in 1563 Parliament passed an Act to stop the practice, since the "coillis continuallie caryit furth of this realme" in ballast "geevis occassioun of maist exhorbitant derth, and scantiness of fewall within the samin." By this time the deeper driving of mines had produced a drainage problem, and mine after mine had been abandoned as waterlogged. In some Lothian pits to-day up to 2000 gallons of water is raised to the surface every minute, but in the sixteenth and seventeenth centuries the only method of fighting these floods was to dam the slanting shaft with clay and "lave" the water gathering there by means of scoops. The chain-and-bucket system provided a solution, motive power being supplied by a horse gin or by harnessing a stream to work a water-wheel, but if a bolt in the chain gave way chain and buckets crashed to destruction at the pit-bottom, a costly loss. As an alternative, at some pits drains were dug for great distances from the coal-face to some outlet at a lower level, perhaps on the sea-shore. Early in the eighteenth century, however, Andrew Wauchope of Edmonstone introduced a steam pumping engine in the Lothians, at a cost of £1007.11s.4d exclusive of the engine-house.

The mounting costs of winning coal had troubled the proprietors fully a century earlier than this. What must surely be one of the earliest examples on record of a coalowners' association took place at Fawside Castle, near Inveresk, when Janet Lawson known by courtesy as Lady Fawside invited to dinner half a dozen other coalowners in the Lothian district, among them the Earl of Winton and the Master of Elphinstone. After dinner, the seven of them discussed the situation and decided to raise the price of coal from 3s per load to 4s, agreeing not to lower this price without the consent of all parties. The Privy Council responded by ordering them to return to the old price, but the coalowners protested and the sequel was something like a Royal Commission on the difficulties in the Lothian coal-heughs, which resulted in the fixing of the load price at 3s. 4d.

The water problem which made the winning of coal so hazardous and costly in the Lothian pits bred a great deal of skill and ingenuity. The *Statistical Account* describes the disastrous state of the industry in Duddingston parish in the middle of the eighteenth century, when the low-level collieries were ruined by an inflow of water from the conduit from some more elevated works further inland. The Earl of Abercorn installed a " powerful engine," pumping from a depth of over 300 feet, and when this was overwhelmed by flooding in 1790 a still more powerful engine had to be employed, but only small portions of the upper seams were workable. Parts of the county must be riddled with water-levels, the drains used to draw off the water to the Esk, the Tyne and other streams, and as many of them bore through stone for most of the way it has been estimated that the cost in some cases must have been as high as £10,000 or even £20,000. In the preface to that strange book, *Satan's Invisible World Discovered*, George Sinclair lauds the ingenuity of the Lothian coal managers in the time of Charles II : " What running of mines and levels ; what piercing of falls ! What cutting of impregnable Rocks, with more difficultie than Hannibal cutting the Alps. What Deep Pits and fire-holes are digged. What diligence to prevent damps, which kill men and beasts in a moment. What contriving of pillars for supporting houses and Churches which are undermined ! What floods of water run thorow the Labyrinths, for several miles, by a free Level, as if they were conducted by a guide." It is true this is all meant to flatter the Earl of Winton, to whom the book is dedicated, but it is a just tribute to the early coal-winners, all the same.

I have already mentioned that by 1606 conditions had become so unpleasant that the Parliament had to tie the miners to their jobs. The subsequent serfdom of the Lothian miners is notorious. The immediate occasion of the Act of 1606 is itself black enough, for a miner called John Henry had wilfully set fire to the coalheugh of Fawside out of " evill will " against the proprietor, and since the law counted this treason Henry was hanged at the Mercat Cross of Edinburgh and his severed head sent out to be exhibited at Fawside. After 1606 no collier could leave without a testimonial from his employer, and if he did so leave the employer could have him brought back. There are many cases on record of fugitives being detected, thrown into prison and sent back. There are also advertisements in newspapers of the

The ornate seventeenth-century cross at Prestonpans

Potato grading on one of the rich farms of East Lothian

times notifying the sales of collieries together with all the machinery, houses and " coal-bearers," illustrating how the men were bought and sold with the pit in which they worked. The man who put an end to this was Henry Dundas, Viscount Melville, himself a son of Lord Arniston and a man who knew the colliery districts of the Lothians. The Dundas Act of 1799 pointed to the miners' bondage and declared them free from servitude ; yet the evil was by no means ended in the Lothians, where several collieries ran what was called the long-contract system, whereby colliers bound themselves to work for a year for a specified bounty money, payable at the end of the year, and only if the collier behaved himself "in a quiet and peaceable manner." The worst feature of this chapter in mining history was the use of female and child labour, and when at last, as late as 1840, a Commission inquired into the matter, conditions in the Lothians were found to be worse than anywhere else in Scotland. Passing through Newtongrange or Rosewell to-day, with their ambitious football grounds and the crops of television aerials on the house-roofs, it is hard to believe that only a little more than a hundred years ago the mining community hereabouts was a caste apart, living in hovels shared with the pigs and poultry and with the bed-clothes as black as the filthy floors. The Commissioners, coming from the capital of an Empire which had made itself the champion of anti-slavery throughout the world, were aghast at what they found. The colliers were a species of troglodyte, or of untouchable, marked by the permanent blackness which came from a fixed belief that washing weakened the back, shunned by all other labourers. But the case of the women and children was worse. Children dragged the coal from the face to the pit-bottom in primitive hutches, along dark, low tunnels without rails, or in some cases the women carried the coal in baskets all the way from the face to the surface. To reach the surface they had to climb a crude, wooden turnpike stair up the pit-shaft, or a thick-runged ladder, and Hugh Miller relates that at Niddrie mill it was estimated these women daily carried the equivalent of one hundredweight from sea-level to the top of Ben Lomond, often weeping like children on the last stages of their climb, and immediately afterwards singing with glee as they descended again into the depths with an empty creel. An Act of Parliament in 1842 put an end to all female labour in the mines, but the women had so accepted the practice that another two years passed before it completely ceased.

This prohibition of women "bearers" was thought at first to be a threat to the mining industry in the Lothians. In the early part of the nineteenth century the industry had already lagged far behind its competitors in Lanarkshire. Partly this was due to the steepness of the workings and, no doubt, to the wetness of some pits ; but the main reason was the demand of the iron and shipbuilding industries of the Clyde, which had no parallel in the east. As a result, the coal distribution trade in the Edinburgh district was antiquated, and coal prices in the capital were much heavier than in Glasgow. Deliveries between the Lothian pits and the city were by means of pathetic, shallow little carts drawn by ill-conditioned horses which could bring no more than perhaps 12 cwts. in a load. The total annual output of the Lothians just before female and child labour came under investigation was about 390,000 tons. In the end the prohibition probably did more than anything else to hasten modernisation. Men would never have been found to take on the drudgery which had been performed by their womenfolk, and within a few years rails were being laid in the main tunnels and ponies were introduced as the means of traction, so that within a generation output had risen to well over three-quarters of a million tons.

The Lady Victoria pit at Newbattle led all others in the Lothians at the end of the nineteenth century. Its gleaming engines were the most powerful, its tunnels were trimly bricked between supporting steel ribs. Output in some Lothian pits rose gradually to 1000 or 1500 tons in a seven-hour day, even where coal had to be brought two miles and more from the face to the pit-bottom. From 1900 on the pace of development doubled and re-doubled. Total output rose from something over two million tons in a year to well over four million tons at the beginning of the First World War, and by that time mechanisation had made a distinct contribution to the result. The face of this part of the Lothians was, of course, changed. The coal-bearing area is not large, and the eruption of pit after pit, with gibbet-like headgear black against the grey dawn and the dusk, scarred a countryside which had been beautiful. "Miners' rows" sprang up at place after place, primitive and unlovely. They were rightly condemned in the twenties, and new sorts of house with what are called modern conveniences grew up around villages such as Arniston and Newtongrange, Ormiston and Pencaitland, Pathhead and Tranent. In a few places cottages with some real character were designed ; but most of the new " rows " offset their advantages with a monotony which was no advance on the monotony of the old, and although pithead baths and miners' institutes had transformed the social outlook of the people of this once-black spot, it has continued ever since to jar the susceptibilities of strangers. Added to the black bings and pitheads now are a number of areas of temporary desolation. They are the open-cast sites, which burst open rural quietude which still lurks around such spots as Pathhead and claw down deep through the brown subsoil, wrenching away the face of the countryside and exposing its vitals, leaving one with just that feeling of sickened wonder at a rape of Nature which one used to get when coming upon a bomb-crater in a familiar meadow during the war. It so happens that the folds and faults of the Carboniferous strata hereabouts produce many outcrops of coal. Ten sites opened up in the Lothians since the later years of the war have yielded something like one million tons. It is only fair to say that when the coal is exhausted these open-cast sites are restored at least to a state in which they can recover their old fertility and agricultural productivity.

At Polton, the Bilston Burn joins the North Esk, coming to meet it by way of the pretty dell of Bilston Glen. The Glen, however, is undergoing grim if inevitable changes. Why such changes should come about anyone with a little geological training could have recognised by a glance at the black cracks in the carpet of the glen at its upper end, for the black cracks were exposures of the coal-bearing strata—the Edge Coals for which this district is noted. And now the Burn is piped in concrete tunnels, and the debris from a pit is filling up the Glen. The new Bilston Glen colliery indeed may be taken as a symbol of contemporary developments in the Lothian coal basin. Coal is a deceptive industry, and there is often not a great deal to show on the surface for immense advances affecting the economy of the whole country. This colliery when completed will have the group

of simple functional buildings which make the Comrie pit over in
Fife by no means an eyesore, especially in its setting of grass
plots and flower beds with a fountain or two, and there is
certainly small hint of the 7 million pounds which this, like
neighbouring pits of its class, are expected to cost in capital
outlay. One understands the figure a little better when one
realises that this one sinking is to exploit an underground area of
four square miles stretching under the North Esk valley, more
than a mile away from the pit-shaft itself. In this area there are
about a hundred million tons of workable coal, mostly at great
depths, and the shaft, or rather the twin shafts, of the Bilston
Glen pit are to go vertically to a depth of 2500 feet, and two
" horizons," consisting of networks of mines and air-tunnels,
will reach out eastwards into the rich seams of the Carboniferous
Limestone groups. The aim is an output of 40 cwts. per man-
shift over a span of a century, so that the planning and equipment
of this costly enterprise must necessarily be first-rate. The main
shaft is devised to accommodate four multi-deck cages, each able
to raise 9 tons of coal through the 2500 feet in less than two
minutes, and the mine cars and machinery are all of the latest
type. Not the least impressive feature is a colossal air shaft, in
the cross-section of its upper part looking like the nave of a small
church, designed to circulate fresh air to the remotest underground workings miles from the pit-bottom and to drive used and
foul air back to the surface. It should be mentioned, incidentally, that dangerous gases are of rare occurrence in the Lothian
coalfield. In some pits there is actually no ban on carrying an
open flame. Water is the chief hazard in these workings, especially perhaps water which has gathered in disused galleries of
old workings, which at the vast depths has been encountered at
a pressure as high as 700 lbs. to the square inch. Portions of the
area are now honeycombed with workings, old and new, and
sometimes when the highly-compressed water is pumped off
the unsupported roofs of old galleries collapse, with consequent
subsidences above and disturbances of goods and chattels in housing schemes which are like the effects of earthquakes.

The second major scheme of the Coal Board in this area,
however, illustrates even more dramatically the drive to tap and
exploit the great hidden resources of the Lothians. This is the

The new colliery at Bilston Glen, designed to mine the rich seams which lie 2,500 feet below the surface

Interior of Roslin Chapel with the Prentice Pillar (left)

Monktonhall colliery, two miles north of Dalkeith. The Lothians coalfield is an enormous basin, with the sides rising more or less sharply to east and west and outcropping as the Edge Coals already mentioned more than once. It is largely this shallow fringe of Edge Coals on which mining enterprise has spent itself from the days of the monks of Newbattle down to the great depression of the thirties, when truckloads of thousands of tons sometimes lay awaiting a buyer and incurring demurrage in the sidings until the birds nested among the coals. The expansion of industry in the past quarter of a century, and especially since the Second World War, has changed the picture. Now there can never be too much coal. But the shallower workings of the area are exhausted or on their way to be so, and it is to the deep bed of this enormous basin that prospectors are looking for the fuel to drive the new industries of Scotland. As far below the cornfields around Dalkeith as the Cuillin peaks soar above the surface of Coruisk lie layers of the richest coals in seams no more than three or four feet thick. Despite the rationalisation which has nationalised the industry and the technological revolution which has made the winning of those riches possible, the seams retain—even in the offices of the Coal Board!—the richly-expressive miners' names which seem to smack of the frontier spirit of a Coal Klondike: Little Splint, Peacocktail, Corbie, Carlton, Parrot Hauchielin. It is to such awe-inspiring depths of as much as 3600 feet that the new pits must go, and the twin 24-foot shafts of Monktonhall are being driven right through the ordinary coal measures to the level of 3300 feet. One descends these great shafts at immense speeds, dazed by the metallic roar and by the racing concrete walls, with ear-drum crackling under the mounting pressure, and there is no time to realise that one is hurtling through geological time—through the Millstone Grit and the Upper Limestone to the richly-seamed Limestone coals deposited in an age when the Lothians were more fantastic than the jungles of the Amazon. In these depths more than two thousand men will work when the colliery is fully developed. Up these echoing shafts will come 4000 tons of coal per day. And as at Bilston Glen there are resources enough to keep up this rate of production for a hundred years. There is said to be well over 1000 million tons of coal in reserve, to say nothing of the huge unproved reserves where the measures dip under the Firth of Forth. Here, and across the Firth in Fife, lies the future of the Scottish mining industry. When present plans are carried out, the coal production of the Lothians will rise to a figure of nearly six million tons per year. This is less than the Fife coalfield's target of ten million tons by 1965 ; but its significance is better understood by comparing it with the dramatic shrinkage of output of the great Central Coalfield which, in total, in 1910 produced twenty million tons but by 1965 will probably have been passed by the Lothians. Mining developments of this kind are slow, for the sinking of a shaft to the Carboniferous Limestone levels requires something like five years, and the driving out of the roadways from the pit-bottom as much time again ; but the result is a complete industrial and social change, so that this region of the Lothians is going to alter considerably in character in the next decade. There is already considerable immigration of mining families from the Lanarkshire area. Fortunately it is now recognised that mine-workings need be no more unsightly than any other big industrial plant, so that there are hopes that the attractions of the countryside on Edinburgh's doorstep will not be marred.

Those attractions are both natural and historical. The parishes of Cockpen and Lasswade, and the valley of the North Esk in particular, can be explored with a great deal of profit, although the daily summer tourist traffic between Edinburgh and the Borders passes them by with never a glance.

Cockpen is a little parish of only about four square miles, but has been made famous all over the world by Lady Nairne's rollicking ballad, " The Laird o' Cockpen." The " braw house " of the song was Old Cockpen House, and it lay in pretty surroundings just east of Dalhousie Castle, by the South Esk, but it has disappeared, the lands being united with the Dalhousie estate in 1785. They were forfeited by Mark Carse, the Laird o' Cockpen who sided with Charles II and went into exile with him after the battle of Worcester, and oddly enough they were recovered because the Laird himself had a gift for music. He played the organ, and when the Court took up impoverished exile at The Hague Carse made ends meet by giving lessons on this instrument. As the sequel shows, he must also have whiled away the time for Charles by playing for him on occasions. At the Restoration Carse returned to Scotland, but he could not recover Cockpen from the Cromwellian sympathisers who had been given the confiscated estate. The Laird, however, had an ingenious idea. He went to London, and by some means persuaded the organist of the Chapel Royal to let him play at a service when the King was present. The service over, for " voluntary " he broke into a startling piece, a jolly Scots air known as " Brose and Butter " which Charles had delighted in at The Hague. It stopped the King's exit like a cannon-shot. Charles declared that only one man knew how to play that tune, and ordered the organist to be brought before him. The old music, he declared to Cockpen, "had made his heart dance," to which Cockpen retorted that to make *his* heart dance he would have to have his lands back. Needless to say, his wish was granted. Tradition has it that Carse was the true Laird of the song. If so, his method of wooing the King's favours was subtler than his wooing of Jean McClish of Claverse-ha' Lee, the " penniless lass wi' a lang pedigree "; but what the song does not relate is that the Laird was in the end successful in this venture too, for Jean thought better of her proud rejection. Moreover, she was not altogether penniless, for the marriage united the estates of Cockpen and Claverse-ha' Lee, otherwise known as Barondale, near Newbattle.

Dalhousie Castle, which absorbed Cockpen, bears a deceptively modern look. The nineteenth-century crenellations, and indeed the general, well-cared-for look, mask the fact that the greater part of the castle belongs to the fifteenth century. Originally it was a defensive tower, like Borthwick a few miles to the south-east, but each century has altered or added to it. Fortunately the stone seems always to have been drawn from the same source, probably the Castle Quarry only a short distance away. It is a warm-toned, durable freestone. Much of the interior has been modernised, but the windowless, vaulted prison is preserved, with a pit or dungeon beneath it, the only access a trapdoor. In various places is carved the eagle of the Ramsays and initials of members of the family which has owned Dalhousie from the start. The Ramsays were one of the numerous foreign knightly families whom David I settled in the Lothians. Thereafter the name of Ramsay appears in nearly every great event in Scottish history : at Bannockburn, among the signatures appended to the Declaration of Arbroath, among the slain at Halidon Hill and at Flodden. Sir John became Lord Ramsay for his services to James VI at the Raid of Ruthven, but the Earldom of Dalhousie did not come until 1633, and the pediments of two windows in the castle carry the initials of the first earl and his wife. There follows a succession of distinguished soldiers, and in the mid-nineteenth century appears the first marquis, who made the name of Dalhousie famous in the East by his term as Governor-General. Born in the castle in 1812, the great establisher of the British Raj, whom, on the outbreak of the Mutiny, those who knew longed to see back in office in India for just one hour, died in his castle by the South Esk at the early age of 48, broken in health by his efforts. This most celebrated of viceroys lies buried in the little ruined church of Cockpen, which dates from the thirteenth century. John Knox's brother William, incidentally was for a time minister of this little kirk.

Cockpen as a name rouses a good deal of curiosity, and I feel unconvinced by the derivations given by the dictionaries of place-names. *Coch-pen* or red-hill is offered by one, and *Cnoc beinn* by another, both words meaning "hill," a double emphasis on a feature far from prominent in the landscape of the parish. I much prefer the Rev. J. C. Carrick's suggestion, in his little book about the Dalkeith district. He claims that the proper name of the place is "Gowkpen," or the Cuckoo-Hill, pointing out in support that there is a Gowkshill in the neighbourhood and that Penicuik a little further up the Esk is simply the words transposed into the form Pen-i-gowk. Gowk is of course Scots for cuckoo, as every first-of-April perpetrator of "huntigowk" pranks should know, and it is likely enough that the bird haunts the wooded dells of the Esk as early as anywhere in the county.

It must be confessed that the mining industry has made something like a desert of great tracts of the country between the two Esks. The pitheads themselves are not really responsible for the dreariness. One sees them on the skyline here and there, but they are not obtrusive features of the landscape and, as I have said earlier, the newer erections such as those at the Bilston Glen colliery are trim and not unattractive. No : the dreariness seems to be due to two things—firstly, a curious unbalance and unease which extensive undermining of a countryside sometimes produces, and secondly, the blight of hurried housing. The first is difficult to define. However, anyone slowly following the road from Inveresk through Dalkeith and south-westwards by way of Rosewell cannot help being aware of the change from a cosy and comfortable stability to a stark, raw region which, in spite of good farming land, has some of the nightmare quality of the dustbowl. The wooded denes and ivied walls become barer as one goes; there are warnings of subsidences, and evidence of them in well-bigged walls which have cracked and crumbled; and the very fields themselves after a space seem, to my fancy, to be awaiting disembowelment or the ravishing of their fertility by housing schemes. Scotland's housing problem has, of course, been a desperate one. Like England's, it has been a political issue, and parties have striven for and boasted about a " progress " which may be accountable in terms of roofs for the homeless but all too seldom means an increase in the numbers of real, worthy homes. So it looks to me to be with this busy part of Lasswade parish. Pleasant names of villages such as Bonnyrigg and Rosewell are mocked at by the brick-and-mortar wildernesses which they are becoming, spattered with repetitive designs of no merit, dooming their inhabitants to a dullness of mental outlook symbolised by the television aerials which appear almost before the curtains are up.

And yet a side road leaves Rosewell and in a few hundred yards is winding through fields towards hanging woods under which the North Esk flows through dark pools and over sparkling weirs. The road winds downwards steeply, crosses the stream and twists rapidly upwards again in the reverse direction to the village of Roslin. In turning, it discloses a lovely little valley commanded by high, wooded bluffs and floored with what once were meadows. Yet even here, where nature has bestowed every advantage, man has been obtuse. The Scot is a sentimentalist about his country, but again and again he brands himself as insensible as a steward of its beauties. If Roslin Glen were in another country people would come on pilgrimage to it from far and near, eager to see not only one of the most remarkable medieval monuments in the country but to delight in the seasonal changes of this natural beauty spot. As it is, they build a factory in its meadow, complete with chimney, pay no particular attention to the style of siting of the other buildings in and about the Glen, in short, treat the setting of the Chapel and the Castle as if those two superb fragments of the Scottish heritage mattered no more than a couple of nineteenth-century farm cottages.

The Chapel lies a few hundred yards south of the village of Roslin, on the edge of a high bluff overlooking the Glen, where the North Esk winds among trees. Fine as the site is, the monument which crowns it is like no other church in Britain, mocking at our national austerity with extravagant stone traceries which belong with fierce sunshine and the accents of the Latin south. The aisles and chapels of this little church of St. Matthew—as it was once—are low and unobtrusive, but the choir rises with a loftiness peculiar in such a tiny building, enshrined in a fence of crocketed pinnacles from which spring its supporting buttresses. In point of fact, what we see here is less than half of the projected church. There was to have been a transept—the eastern wall of it exists—and a nave so lofty and so daring in its vaulting that doubt has been thrown on its feasibility. At Roslin, however, there is no urge to lament what never was. So skilful were the builders in what they did complete that the passing of five centuries has left their work in a perfect state. What is not always appreciated is the perfection of proportion and line, for if one can dim the extravagant detail with half-closed eyes the church will still seem a lovely thing, and even in this one is aware of a strong originality.

Yet undoubtedly this originality is most marked in the adoption of fantastic ornament. At the time of building England had attempted nothing so extravagant. Indeed in all northern Europe there is nothing extravagant in just this way ; and the odd thing is that in detail the intricate ornament is not before its time, but rather casts a backward glance at the Middle Ages, at the Dark Ages even and their preoccupation with the world of bestiaries. All this can be seen most vividly inside the church. Professor Hannah described it as being like woods bursting into song, for every capital, every cornice and projection, is fretted with foliaceous detail. There are sacred figures, if one looks for them ; but the dominant note is that gorgeous medieval overspill of creativeness which seizes upon everything, fact or fancy,

irrespective of biblical or ritualistic meaning. The vaulting of
the aisles is so intricate in its close-knit patterns of leafy forms
that it recalls Arabian screens or Indian filigree, and it has
reminded at least one serious commentator of Hindu temples.
There is a rectangular panel treatment of a seven-leaf form which
is quite novel and especially lovely. Even the shafts of the
columns themselves are carved with the greatest intricacy. The
most famous of them is of course the South Pier, known as the
Prentice Pillar, with its spiral garlands on a deeply-channelled
shaft, capital and base being sculptured with exceptional brilliance.
The story goes that the master-sculptor went to Rome on a
pilgrimage to look for inspiration, that in his absence an appren-
tice carved the pillar, only to meet his death at the hand of his
master on his return ; but this sort of tale is not uncommon—
Rouen has its pillar too—and it is clear enough that it was no
' prentice hand which carved this masterpiece with its consum-
mate symbolism—the coiling worm at the base gnawing at the
tendrils creeping upwards towards the light. This characteristic
medieval concept is paralleled by the leering demon at the meeting-
place of the arcades in the south-east corner, and above all by the
danse macabre in the eastern aisle, with its procession of folk in
all walks of life, each partnered by a grisly skeleton.

I have never quite been able to understand Professor Hannah's
claim that Roslin is, in its essential features, Scottish. The choir
is perhaps borrowed from Glasgow ; but the plan of the chapel
is unique, and Hannah's belief that the ornament is " Caledonian "
is, I think, derived from his impression that the intertwining
patterns are Celtic. The treatment of the more elaborate piers
suggests Spain and Portugal, the aisle vaulting is Burgundian.
On the other hand, the extravaganza as a whole derives from
nowhere except the ambition of Sir William Sinclair, third Earl
of Orkney, to build a " sumptuous structure " and from the
eclectic mind of his architect or master-mason, whoever he may
have been. The time of the chapel's erection was about 1450.
The Earl lived to complete only the choir. His builders had
come up against one technical problem after another, and it
may be the nave would have defeated them, but the main reason
for the stoppage seems to have been the attitude of his son,
Oliver, who had no mind to spend his fortune in building a

church and so hastily rounded off what had been done with a minimum of expenditure.

Soaring from its wooded bluff, the chapel is romantic enough, and Scott embroidered that romance in the famous group of verses in *The Lay of the Last Minstrel* which tell how the death of a St. Clair is heralded by a sinister red glow which illumines the chapel :

> Blazed battlement and pinnet high,
> Blazed every rose-carved buttress fair—
> So still they blaze, when fate is nigh
> The lordly line of high St. Clair.

In the crypt of the chapel each member of " the lordly line " is said to have been laid " with candle, with book and with bell," without coffin, but " sheathed in his iron panoply." The story goes that when the vault was last opened, the breastplates of twelve barons were found lying in a little dust. Whether the description " breastplates " is an exact one, or merely careless recording, I have no means of knowing, but I recall long ago a discussion with some specialists in armour who thought that a further investigation might be well worth while, although one could hardly hope to see the complete harnesses of twelve generations of St. Clairs.

The home and stronghold of the Sinclairs—St. Clairs—lies just a little further up the Glen. The Esk, babbling idly through sheltered meadowland, meets the precipitous south slope of the Glen and is turned back upon itself, flowing between the wooded slope on the one hand and a high, rocky bluff on the other, looping around this height so that it nearly isolates it. In the days before gunpowder, it would be hard to find a better defensive position. All that was needed was to fortify this height. The perfect entrance to the castle of Roslin has been formed by joining it to the north side of the Glen by means of a bridge which arches some fifty feet above a chasm. Originally this bridge had a timber construction, and the present daring span of masonry, looming so massively, so gigantically, especially in the grey, moist dusk of a spring or autumn evening, dates from the end of the sixteenth century. Much of the rest of the castle belongs to this time, a lofty dwelling which sheltered the inner courtyard

Hawthornden Castle

The Pentland Hills, south-west of Edinburgh

from the east. To the west and north are fifteenth-century work, and it is recorded that Sir William, who succeeded to the Sinclair title in 1417 " builded also the foreworke that looks to the north-east." Below the great domestic block the already steep rock-face has been artificially scarped so that cliff and masonry are one, forming a tremendous, unscalable wall.

A little further up the Glen, where the road bends round sharply to climb to Roslin village after crossing the stream, a startling notice shows up under the shade of the trees. It reads : GUNPOWDER MILLS—NO ADMITTANCE. The leafy seclusion of the place, silent but for the cooing of wood-pigeons and the trilling of a thrush, lends an even more sinister air to the notice. This is the entrance to the oldest gunpowder mill in the country, or so it was until 1954, when the undermining of the Glen by the quest for coal caused subsidences which might have added to the dangers of the factory, which was therefore closed down. Enough remains to show that a gunpowder mill could be as much a part of the rural scene as a flour mill. The various buildings were set down among the woods of the Glen in 1790, just before the French Revolution broke, and outwardly they were not altered a great deal during the span of their existence, so that the making of gunpowder became almost a rural industry. Indeed, the charcoal—which every schoolboy knows to be one of the three ingredients required—was for generations made from alders growing on the banks of the Esk, which also lent its strength to turn the mill to grind the powder. No doubt the seclusion was from the start one of the advantages of the place, and some of the scattered buildings were hunched against the uprising banks of the dell, overhung by ancient trees, to mini-mise the effect of accidents, just as in explosives works of to-day. On a face of rock is carved the date " 1815," and this is said to be a record of the fact that Roslin powder was used at Waterloo. The processes changed little ; only the use to which the powder was put changed. This black-powder had long ceased to be used for guns before the mill closed, and latterly the customers were shale and slate quarriers, who liked it for what the trade rather euphemistically calls its gentle, heaving action. The most vital, and perhaps most dangerous process in the preparation is the grinding up of the three ingredients to a fine powder, and at

Roslin this was done by means of massive steel edge-runner mills, five-ton pestles working in a huge mortar. The original mills worked by a paddle-wheel were still in order in 1954, but four others were powered by an enormous beam-engine installed in 1863 but probably half-a-century older than that. Those early beam-engines have an epic look, even when transplanted to the Science Museum in London, and the Roslin ones in action must have recalled Blake's "dark, satanic mills." So unstable is the powder when being milled that an old nail or a few grains of sand crushed by the steel could set off the spark that would ignite the powder and bring disaster. Right to the end there was always a searcher at the gate of the mill, to make sure that no one brought matches inside or similar combustibles, and it is said that in the old days the hirsute men who appear in the old, faded staff photographs even had their beards searched for matches. It is one of my regrets that I never had an opportunity to see in action what is perhaps the only chemical works which could lay claim to be called picturesque. Its beam-engines, its giant scales for weighing out the ingredients, its kegs—made by the mill's own cooper—and even the somewhat disconcerting process of hand-breaking the cakes of gunpowder with a heavy wooden mallet preparatory to "corning" must have produced an atmosphere, a queer sense of drama, hard to find in the impersonal factories of to-day. The mill in its way belonged to the age of craftsmanship, and many of its workers were faithful to it, generation after generation, and seemed to have loved its rural setting and the wild life of the woods about it much as the weaver-poets of Paisley did their countryside.

A mile below Roslin the valley of the North Esk narrows to a gorge spectacular in the Highland rather than in the Border manner. Thick, hanging woods clothe its rocky walls, the roots of the trees clinging like claws to ledge and fissure, and on the right bank for a distance there are bare sandstone cliffs. At one point these dominate the river below, formed in a great wedge or promontory. Surmounting this promontory is Hawthornden Castle, the comparatively modern version of an old strong-place which still exists in the ruins of a fifteenth-century tower and hall. To the tower is attached the present Castle which in the main dates from the seventeenth century, precariously perched on the cliff's edge and looking like an upthrust of the rock itself. An inscription over the doorway dates it to the year 1638, and the initials S.W.D. commemorate Sir William Drummond, the poet, the lines of the inscription recording that Drummond, by the bounty of Heaven, restored the house for himself and his descendants "that he might rest in honourable leisure." In itself the house is interesting, but perhaps its most interesting feature is the series of caves in the rock below it—famous caves which have been described by such travellers as Pennant and no doubt used as refuges in far-off times. The *Scotichronicon* relates that Sir Alexander Ramsay made the caves his headquarters in the fourteenth century, issuing with his band of fighting men from time to time to raid the English border ; and he seems to have established there a sort of battle-training school to which all young men of spirit and of noble family went to learn his commando tactics. Certainly he could have picked no better practice-ground, and it would be hard to find a better hide-out. The caves are directly under the Castle and go far into the rock. They are on two levels and there are many chambers. There are fireplaces, seats and cupboard accommodation, and a window or two giving on to the chasm below. There is also a deep well-shaft which would keep the Castle and the caves supplied with water for any length of time. Pennant, understandably found more to admire in "the solemn and picturesque walks cut along the summits, sides and bottoms of this beautiful den," with its red precipices, its trees, its grotesque rocks and the distant views of the Pentland hills.

Tradition links Hawthornden with Robert the Bruce. In the caves is a passage called the King's Gallery, and there are also a King's Bed-Chamber, a King's Dining Room and a King's Guard Room, while the *Statistical Account* draws attention to a marble slab-table in the "lobby" of the Castle on which lies "a large two-handed and two-edged sword, said to have belonged to Robert the Bruce." The compiler is very wisely circumspect, for the great sword is not earlier than the sixteenth century ; but nevertheless it is one of the most remarkable swords of its kind, for it is the only known claymore with four quillons, or cross-guards.

There is probably better reason for associating Hawthornden with King Robert III, whose queen was Arabella Drummond. The Drummonds have been in possession of the place for a very long time, and Sir William was not the only distinguished member of the family. It is Sir William who is meant, however, when the name of Drummond of Hawthornden is uttered. Here, under a sycamore tree, Drummond greeted Ben Jonson with the often-quoted words :

Welcome, welcome, Royal Ben !

to which Jonson at once retorted :

Thank ye, thank ye, Hawthornden !

Drummond was in fact a considerable poet. Burns is probably responsible for the impression that Scots verse, especially vernacular verse, is essentially of the people, but earthy as much of the verse may be gentle blood has produced far more than a fair share of it, from Barbour and Lyndsay to Lady Grizel Baillie. But Drummond wrote only in English. He was the best Scottish poet of the seventeenth century, yet he spent many years abroad and his literary background is Spenser and the Italians. Jonson when he visited him told him that " his verses were too much of the schooles." In the Civil War, as might be expected, he was on the side of Charles and Episcopacy. The mood of his finest work, the *Cypresse Grove*, is philosophical, and does not breathe the countryside in which he lived, as so much Scottish verse does—in spite of the striking beauty of the hanging woods of Hawthornden. He is buried in the family mausoleum in the grounds of the ruined old parish kirk of Lasswade.

Lasswade has more literary associations than one might look for in the matter-of-fact village of to-day. Near Drummond lies John Clerk of Eldin. He was hardly a literary man in the ordinary sense, but he wrote a successful book which, it has been claimed, revolutionised British naval warfare at a critical time and made possible the victories of Nelson and the other great admirals of his time. The odd thing is that John Clerk was not a sailor and had no practical knowledge of seamanship, but his ideas seem to have ended the stalemate that frustrated the British navy in the second half of the eighteenth century. He married a sister

Swanston, Robert Louis Stevenson's village

Corstorphine Kirk

of Robert Adam, and a son became the judge, Lord Eldin. Around the time of John Clerk's death Walter Scott began married life with his young French bride in a cottage in Dalkeith, the humble start to a romance that was to end at Abbotsford. Lasswade was well-placed for those rides deep into the Border country which stored Scott's mind with the lore on which he was to build his fame. He was soon a welcome visitor in all the great houses of the neighbourhood . . .

> . . . To Auchendinny's hazel shade,
> And haunted Woodhouselee.
>   Who knows not Melville's beechy grove
> And Roslin's rocky glen,
>   Dalkeith which all the virtues love
> And classic Hawthornden?

A few years more and the village streets were being haunted by a much stranger writer. About 1840 Thomas de Quincey began to journey out from his house in Lothian Street in Edinburgh to the villa between Lasswade and Polton where he was to spend much of the last twenty years of his odd life. He wandered around Lasswade a great deal in his absent way, often sleeping under the stars, his wife and family having no idea of his whereabouts, and many a story was current of how people turned him from their doors under the impression he was a vagrant or a pedlar of stationery.

Auchendinny House and Melville Castle, mentioned in the lines of Scott above, are both notable in their ways. Auchendinny is perhaps chiefly remarkable because it is the last house built by Sir William Bruce, and also the smallest. It was completed about 1707, when the architect was 77, for John Inglis, an Edinburgh lawyer. The plan of the house is familiar enough: a central block flanked by outflung pavilions. About the end of the eighteenth century Auchendinny was occupied for a few years by a celebrated partner in the firm of Inglis, Henry Mackenzie, a forerunner of Scott and Stevenson in the Scottish practice of combining law with literary work. His best known work is, of course, *The Man of Feeling*. Melville Castle lies a little farther down the Esk. Its principal association is with Henry Dundas, Viscount Melville, the lofty column to whose memory in St. Andrew's Square, Edinburgh, yearly causes so many tourists to expose the ignorance of the capital's citizens in the matter of her major monuments; but the castle was in fact bought by Dundas's father-in-law as a gift for his daughter. Dundas was one of the Dundases of Arniston, and had his schooling in Dalkeith. His brilliant political career need not be recounted here, but it is odd and interesting that if John Clerk of Eldin prepared the way for the victorious strategy of the British navy, this still more distinguished son of the parish of Lasswade built up the navy into a fighting machine capable of carrying out that strategy efficiently. The money for the erection of the Melville monument in Edinburgh was to a large extent subscribed by naval officers who held him in high regard.

The basin of the two Esk rivers, bounded by the Moorfoots and the Pentlands, has been one of the choicest rural districts in the kingdom. All within a day's ride of the capital, it was one of the old royal hunting grounds. Before pit-bings and mill chimneys and, worst of all, graceless housing colonies came to infest it, the country lying between the two streams hidden in their twisting little valleys must have been an enchanting patchwork of farms and forests. There are still pretty spots, but most of them are nooks by the rivers where the wider scene is shut off by over-arching trees and woody crags. For generations it has been a week-end playground for the citizens of Edinburgh. For a time it was almost too easy of access, as litter in some of its loveliest dells and meadows demonstrated. The litter now is of another sort and on a larger scale, but as a playground it has probably given place to the more distant places which speedy transport now brings within reach. The least-spoilt portion is the upper reaches of the North Esk, which include the scene of Allan Ramsay's lovely pastoral, *The Gentle Shepherd*; but the stream there is more of a hill burn and part of the Pentland picture so that it belongs more properly in the chapter which follows.

CHAPTER FIVE

Hills and Mills

THE PENTLANDS are the most interesting range of hills coming within the borders of the Lothians. Partly this is sentimental. The Pentlands personify the Lothians to anyone returning home from far places, and they have an unmistakable profile possessed by none of the other ranges, although their expression varies with the mood of him who sees them. Coming out of the north with its far greater hills, one feels these to be almost comically domestic, like some well-liked feature of the household suddenly seen as pathetically inadequate after the scale and dignity of princely mansions, and the dimpled pate of Allermuir and the buxom curve of Caerketton look hardly more romantic than the shale-bings in the foreground ; but after the toy fields and suburbias of England the Pentland ridge has all the remoteness of the High Grampians, and it seems impossible that a great city lies hidden just beyond. What makes the Pentlands so interesting is that both impressions are perfectly valid. One succeeds the other, endlessly, even to those who live in the shadow of the hills themselves, as I do.

Subjective feelings apart, the Pentlands do span two worlds. They begin in the west as a wilderness of watersheds, where man's foot falls too rarely to disturb the curlews, and only ten or a dozen miles away in the east they end, believe it or not, within the bounds of one of the Edinburgh Corporation's public parks ! But they have a special character of their own. Traditionally one of the barriers between north and south, cut only by a drove-road or two, they were a frontier and battlefield from the time of the Picts down to the day of the Covenanters. To-day they are almost an economic unit, if a declining one, with very much the same sort of things going on along the two little river valleys which drain them, one to the south of them, the other to the north. And above all, they and their little river valleys are enfolded in the same mantle of romantic sanctity and of nostalgic memory.

The western fastnesses of the Pentlands are the meeting point of Peeblesshire and Lanarkshire with the Lothians, and they are as lonely a region as one may meet with in almost any part of these islands. The hills are not high, nor are they dramatic in form or in grouping ; but almost the whole area is a sheep-run, large tracts of it boggy or partially reclaimed, and on a lowering spring evening when a lurid light colours thousands of acres of dead grass bleached by winter there is an air of desolation which the heathery Highland country rarely matches. As one might expect, the human stories which cling to this region are as sparse as the vegetation. One human trail only has left its mark across the wilderness. This climbs the hills and crosses them by means of a shallow pass known as the Cauldstaneslap, a depression between two hills, the East and the West Cairns. There are various unsatisfactory derivations of this name, among them Milne's " slap with a stone in it on the north side of a hill," almost as unconvincing a derivation of a name as can be found in any dictionary. " Slap " is of course simply a gap. One glance at this great cleft itself and the rest of the name falls into place. Through the Slap lay the main drove road from the Highlands to the markets of the south, and although history as we read it in the documented books may not have flowed much over this bleak route, the sort of history which men tell to one another by the winter fireside is thick upon the ground. The drovers herded their cattle beasts by this way from Uphall and Midcalder in the north. They " stanced " them in meadows below the pass itself, and men not so long dead remembered the snow reddened by hundreds of hooves bruised on the turnpikes, as Dr. Haldane has recorded in his fine book on the drove roads. Many a foray there was upon the resting herds of nights, no doubt ; but the dangers of the Cauldstaneslap, the real dangers, lay in wait for the drovers returning northward with their hard-won English money about them. Sometimes the drovers were murdered. This was the country of the moss-troopers, and although in Cairns Castle there was a Warden of the Slap there must have been little he could do against those fierce bands of outlaws slipping here and there in the dark among the folds of the hills.

The drovers' best shield was their own toughness, and tough they certainly were, living on meal and whisky and sleeping among their own beasts when the sun went down.

The drove road over the Cauldstaneslap is a sort of back-entrance to the Lothians, and the East and West Cairns are the gateposts, for the county boundary runs across the tops of the twin hills. Both summits are about 1840 feet. From either, one looks south or west into wild, rolling country. Eastward again, yet within the Lothian boundary, are more baldish, grassy tops dappled by the travelling clouds : the East and West Kips, Braid Law, Scald Law and others. At their feet, to the south, flows the North Esk, presently winding among fields and trees which are the scene of that lovely old pastoral comedy, *The Gentle Shepherd* . . .

> Beneath the south side of a craigy bield,
> Where crystal springs their halesome waters yield,
> Twa youthfu' shepherds on the gowans lay,
> Tenting their flock ae bonny morn of May.
> Poor Roger granes till hollow echoes ring ;
> But blither Patie likes to laugh and sing.

This charming eighteenth-century work by Allan Ramsay has had an imaginative revival at the Edinburgh Festival, where a mid-night performance by candlelight, the candles carried by powdered footmen, was on one occasion graced by Royalty ; but the true setting of the play is the estate of Newhall. Indeed, it continued to be very popular down into the earlier part of the nineteenth century. The weavers of the Esk villages were brought up on its lines, and there seems to have been some jealousy about the play's associations, one district vying with another for the credit of being Ramsay's original. The Carlops players were especially noted, performing in barns in various villages as far off as Penicuick and even Peebles, to which the players travelled in a be-ribboned cart with gaily-decorated horse.

Penicuik itself, the parish town of this part, is a pleasant town without being distinguished or picturesque. It still has traces however of the aura of the great family of the Clerks of Penicuik. Penicuik House itself is now, alas, a roofless ruin, but its façade with Ionic portico in the Palladian style still has immense dignity and is a fitting monument to the man who designed it. This man was Sir John Clerk, the 3rd Baronet (1676-1755). Scotland has not had many wealthy and well-informed patrons of the arts, and Sir John might be claimed as the greatest of them. To his father's annoyance, he broke off his law-schooling at Leyden to visit Italy, and he spent a long time there, studying the ruins diligently and acquiring considerable skill with his pencil, studying music under Pasquini and Corelli, and absorbing the immense knowledge of the classics from which he got such great delight throughout his life. Sir John personifies that great eighteenth-century school of Scotsmen the twin foundations of whose lives were the Bible and the Latin authors, although they remained ruggedly Scots at the core. He was man-of-the-world enough to serve as a gentleman of the bed-chamber to Duke Cosimo III of Florence, yet never ceased to regard porridge and cream as *nutrimentum divinum*. His law studies were evidently sufficiently advanced for him to be called to the Scots bar shortly after his return from Italy, and his interest in all forms of human knowledge from land improvement and coal-mining to the study of antiquities continued throughout his life. A monument to his interest in ancient things has survived in the queer dome which balances the steeple over the entrance to the stables at Penicuik House, for this is a replica of a structure called Arthur's O'on, a Roman temple near Falkirk destroyed to build a weir over the River Carron, to the indignation of Sir John and his friend Dr. Stukely. He may have had the same building in mind when he drew the design for his fantastic domed library with Turkish bath, never built, but the actual model for this was clearly the Pantheon in Rome, whose cool mystery and coffered dome, peopled with the ghosts of the great from Hadrian to Raphael, doubtless held Sir John in its spell as it does all visitors. One should visit Penicuik House with the volume of his *Memoirs* to dip into. The parklands, the lovely ornamental lake with its wooded shores are in its pages in process of creation, and one can re-live the anguish of Sir John over the death in childbirth of his beautiful, eager first wife. One of the glories of the house before the fire which destroyed it were the ceiling paintings by Runciman in the Great Ossian Hall, depicting scenes from the legends of Ossian. Sir John was Runciman's patron and sent him to study in Italy, although the works at Penicuik were commissioned by the 4th Baronet, Sir James. It is said that the unwonted exertions of painting the ceiling lying on his back were the cause of the painter's death. The *Statistical Account* comments that " pieces so executed cannot, of course, be expected to display the highest perfection of the art," ignoring Michelangelo's achievement on the ceiling of the Sistine Chapel !

Perhaps even more in the past than now, Penicuik has been a parish of tinkling streams running in shadowed dells. Extensive drainage in the nineteenth century must have lessened the volume of water which drew to it numerous mills. The excellence of the water supply made it a famous centre of the paper-making industry, and it has continued to be so down to the present day. The huge Valleyfield mill seems to be the oldest of its kind in the country. It was founded in 1709. But like enough there were paper mills in Penicuik long before that, for the first prerequisite for the birth of paper mills long ago was the proximity of a centre of printing, and Edinburgh expanded rapidly as a printing centre from the day when Walter Chepman and Androw Myllar collaborated at the beginning of the sixteenth century. By 1763 there were three mills in or about Penicuik, with an annual output of 6400 reams ; but by 1773 there were twelve, producing 100,000 reams by which time there were about 27 printing works in the capital to feed. It was just after this time that Charles Cowan bought the Valleyfield mill, and there began one of those expansions of an industry into an institution which were to form one of the better aspects of Victorian industrialism. The development of paper-making marched with the development of better conditions for the men and women who made the paper. About the end of the century the beater was introduced to macerate the rag-pulp fibres, and by 1859 the Valleyfield alone had 21 beaters, and Charles Cowan had already sent Gladstone a sample of a new wheat-straw paper which he had devised to meet the growing shortage of rags ; and at the same time a school had been opened to teach the three R.s to illiterate mill employees, while Cowan's grandson had been returned to Parliament as member for Edinburgh against such a famous candidate as Macaulay. Paper-milling had ceased to be a rural industry ! It did not, however, cease to be a craft, and in this sense the great mills scattered along the North Esk and Water of Leith valleys are not out of keeping with the fields and farms around them. Mechanisation, as we should call it to-day, began early in the nineteenth century with the inventions of Fourdrinier, and the *Statistical Account* is already remarking on the fact that the five machines at Penicuik " which require the attendance of only one man and two lads, accomplish as much nearly as 30 men and lads could perform formerly by the vat." Yet the achievements of the different mills, with the same machines and the same materials, have always been subtly different, in the high-grade papers at least. Perhaps the chief characteristic of Scottish papers, as distinct from English, is the use of esparto grass, less widely adopted in the south. This crop from the hot plains of North Africa and Spain first went into the boilers at Penicuik in 1860. The abolition of the Paper Duty Tax in the following year unleashed further energy in the mills, whose output rose to ten times what it had been at the beginning of the century. The latest American machinery was installed in 1875—although it should be said that the highly complex machines required for modern paper-making have to a considerable degree been developed in the Lothians, by study of the individual needs of the paper mills there, two of the four firms making such machinery in Britain being in Edinburgh. Now the great mills round which Penicuik has grown are linked with all parts of the world, with branch factories and selling organisations in many of the Commonwealth cities.

The annals of the Clerk family apart, Penicuik has no particular place in history. The slopes and valleys of the hills overlooking it, however, have acquired a rich patina from the past, if a good deal of it is encrusted with legend. This was the Royal hunting-ground of Mount Lothian, best celebrated in the tale of Hold and Help. This tale seems to begin, as most of the hunts did, at the Buck Stane, a huge granite block near Mortonhall Golf Clubhouse, long since within the southern district of Edinburgh. From this stone one morning in the reign of King Robert the Bruce, a great concourse of knights and ladies set off to test the boast of Sir William St. Clair of Roslin that his two hounds, Hold and Help, would catch the white faunch deer which

had eluded the King's hounds, and would do it before the stag
crossed the March Burn. The King must have been nettled by
the fact that Sir William had been ahead of him in the hunt, or he
would never have accepted the wager whereby Sir William staked
his life on success, but success was to bring the winner not only
his life but also the forest of Pentland Moor. Sir William very
nearly lost his wager, for the stag got half-way across the burn to
safety. But there Hold got a grip of him, and Help turned him
back to make an end of him on the bank. The knight's life was
saved, and the King bestowed upon him the entire range of the
Pentlands. At the same time he gave the hand of Sir William's
sister to Randolph de Clerc, and with it the estate of "Pen-
necuik." Then farther east, on the slopes of the Castlelaw Hill,
stands Woodhouselee. The old Woodhouselee is a ruin, once
owned by Hamilton of Bothwellhaugh. After the battle of Lang-
side the house was seized by the favourites of the Regent Moray,
who turned Bothwellhaugh's beautiful wife Margaret out into
the fields, almost naked, together with her newly-born child.
She was driven mad by her treatment, and died. Scott, in his
Ballad of Cadzow Castle, described how her ghost haunted
Woodhouselee . . .

> The wildered traveller sees her glide,
> And hears her feeble voice with awe—

> 'Revenge,' she cries, 'on Moray's pride,
> And woe for injured Bothwellhaugh!

The sequel belongs to history, for Bothwellhaugh was the man
who lay in wait for the Regent Moray behind a window in
Linlithgow High Street and shot him as he passed, afterwards
escaping to France. The ghost of Margaret, carrying the child,
is said to haunt Woodhouselee still.

At the foot of the nearby Carnethy Hill is a stone monument
which is still a regular place of pilgrimage and, obscure as it is
in this wooded glen, commemorates a more significant chapter of
Scottish history than does the far more famous monument to
Prince Charlie at Glenfinnan. The event which it commemorates
is the battle of Rullion Green, fought on 28th November 1666.
It was a very small battle, not much more than a skirmish, but

it brought to an end the Pentland Rising, that ultimate phase of the struggle for the Covenant to which this range of familiar and yet oddly remote little hills has given its name. Here among those hills, beside their bogs and burns and hid in their hollows, took place so many of the " conventicles " at which the adherents of the Covenant, men, women and children, worshipped in secret, their sentries placed in outposts to watch for their persecutors, the King's men, their preachers often masked in case spies and informers were among the worshippers. Those austere and lonely and yet friendly hills are perhaps more closely identified with the Covenanters than any other part of Scotland except Galloway. They are as symbolic of the Scottish spirit as any purple Highland ben. No one has seized upon their significance more surely than R. L. Stevenson, who spent so much of his childhood in their shadow, for this long-haired, velvet-jacketed Bohemian apprehended as few others have done the poetry that mingles with the apparent Philistinism and bigotry of his race. He belongs more intimately with the other side of the hills, as we shall see presently, but here in this glen, the graves of forgotten martyrs before his eyes, the thin, lost cries of the whaups in his ears, he conceived lines which are among the most haunting in Scots poetry. Often enough in those days when even the weakly were not afraid of walking a few rugged miles he seems to have crossed the hills from Swanston to attend the kirk at Glencorse, and no doubt he found time to sit on a stone in the shelter of a fir plantation and let his mind discard all the years back to that November morning in 1666. A grim morning it was for that remnant of the Covenanters, a mere nine hundred men who had struggled from the west through rain and mire with the soldiers on their heels and now looked at a red sun rising on hills white with a heavy overnight fall of snow. Colonel Wallace drew up his half-armed men in a good position to stand against the troops of that hounder of Presbyterianism, Thomas Dalyell of the Binns, who came down in force from the hills to the north. At first the Covenanters resisted well and repulsed the Government troops, but when their left wing was shattered a general charge broke up their positions. Not a great number were killed and night came to cover the flight of the fugitives, but the persecutions which followed have left a dark stain on the times, and of the fifty prisoners from Rullion Green who were cast into the Haddock's Hole and the Tolbooth of Edinburgh, fifteen were hanged and many put to the torture.

A short distance from Rullion Green the Biggar Road crosses the Glencorse Burn at Flotterstone, the starting or finishing point for large numbers of Edinburgh's week-end hill walkers. It has been a pretty little place. At the less popular times it still has considerable attractions. A road winds up the glen for a mile or two, when it hugs the shore of Glencorse Reservoir, an artificial piece of water formed early in the nineteenth century to help supply the city. Like some modern reservoirs, its waters have engulfed an old church, St. Catherine's. Above Glencorse Reservoir, the burn comes out of a narrower glen between Carnethy and the Black Hill. Here the waters are trapped again, this time in the reservoir of Loganlea. Those Pentland reservoirs have been compared with Highland lochs, even by such an authority as Hugh Miller; but the bald, grey-green hog-backs of the Pentlands and the neatly-tended reservoirs themselves bear no more than a superficial likeness to the great lochs of the north. However, the hundreds of Irish labourers have long ago left the hills to their sheep and their peewits, and out of the autumn skies above the wild geese come honking in their tattered V-formations to rest for the night, drawn by the lonely waters.

Curiously lonely too are the moors where the Water of Leith has its source, in spite of the fact that the docks of Leith, where this little river enters the sea, are no more than a good day's walk away. The dark vistas of heather and the black peat-hags might easily be in the midst of Lewis or Sutherland. Here rise a number of streams, although the watershed is so indeterminate that an old minister of Dolphinton claimed that salmon could come up from the Tweed by this way and go down into the Clyde! The hills around have rocky, uncompromising names: Black Law, Craigengar, Garvel Syke. There is no shelter except here and there a boulder or the burn's bank, or the deep heather itself. Yet this is a country where hunted men hid themselves, whether moss-troopers or the little assemblies seeking cover to hold their conventicles, and at least one wounded Covenanter found a known grave in these wastes. The Water of Leith itself rises somewhere in the shadow of the West Cairn and winds through the moors for a mile or two before flowing into the reservoir of Harperrig, a considerable artificial loch which diversifies the otherwise rather bleak scenery on the eastward section of the " Lang Whang," the road to Carnwath and the west. There was no such watery expanse in the wilderness when Sir George Crichton, the Lord High Admiral of Scotland, built the East Cairns Castle at what is now the top end of the loch, and his purpose in those fifteenth-century days was not boating but constituting himself a sentinel in front of the pass of the Cauldstaneslap. This rolling country then went in terror of the wild Scotts and Elliots and Armstrongs. And just as there was a constant illicit traffic from south to north over the ' Slap,' so there was a good deal of dubious traffic from west to east along the route of the Lang Whang : smuggler gangs from Ayrshire and gypsies like Captain William Baillie, who conducted his business in style. A writer of sixty years ago, even, describes this old Lanark Road as virgin white in winter, innocent of wheelmark or of any footprint except the moorcocks ; but the situation has changed, and the road is now one of the twin main highways into the Clyde Valley and Ayrshire, finely engineered, though still a lonely route and only occasionally meeting with cottage or clump of trees. Some of the stopping-places on this old stagecoach route retain their suggestive names : Little Vantage, for instance, and Boll of Bere. A little farther along the road lay the inn called Jenny's Toll, where two resurrection-men took rest and refreshment while the bodies they had stolen from Lanark kirkyard for the anatomists in Edinburgh waited under a load of peats and straw in the cart outside, to be rescued and restored to their graves by a posse of vigilantes from Currie village.

Below Harperrig the Water of Leith winds through a gentle depression which grows rapidly more cultivated as it falls to the east. Where it is joined by the Cock Burn it still has soaring moorland to the right of it, but to the left are fields mingled with wooded policies. From this point the little stream plunges into the first stretch of those winding, wooded dells which lend it so much beauty for the next few miles. But it is no idle stream. From Balerno citywards it works its passage diligently, or did in the days when water was eagerly sought as the motive-power of industry. Three sorts of mill shoulder one another down the Water of Leith, the paper, flour, and snuff mills, and in almost every successive bend of the river there is a mill-lade, though the great wheels are now rusty and weed-bound.

Balerno is the first village into which the Water of Leith flows, and it is at the same time the terminus of a chain of villages along this north skirt of the Pentlands which have largely degenerated into dormitory suburbs of Edinburgh. The villages south of the hills have to some extent at least retained their identities. They are rather less easily accessible, and in such a case as Penicuik the local industry provides some sort of independent life. Balerno has the same sort of industry in the shape of a big paper mill, but its expansion is due to its popularity as a residential area. The name has a curious foreign flavour about it, Italian or Irish, and I have come across no satisfactory derivation of it, but it is said to have been called Barney until some time last century, so that the late Dr. Geddie's suggested translation of the name as " a warm, sheltered place " may not be wide of the mark. At least this description fits. The wooded cleughs about the meeting-place of the Bavelaw Burn and the Water of Leith at Balerno Bridge are snug and pretty, and the village could have been delightful, with its winding, climbing street, if the Scots had been a race with any feeling and talent for developing amenities. As it is, the attractions of Balerno are in its surroundings, especially about the little road which strikes upwards towards Bavelaw and the hills, crossing Balerno Common and Threipmuir Reservoir, dominated by the vast hog-back of the Black Hill. To walk the moor road on a winter afternoon, with a crackle of ice in the ruts, a stink of dung in the air and the whaups crying over Listonshiels, and know that Princes Street is under half-an-hour's car-run away is to appreciate what an extraordinarily fortunate city Edinburgh is. Balerno used to be the terminus of one of the prettiest branch railway lines in the country, the stub carriages of the little train weaving their way through a great variety of scenery as they followed the Water of Leith's course, and hundreds of hill-walkers used to pour out on to the cinder platform every week-end. I think Sir Winston Churchill must have been the last man to use this little country platform, and I watched him stump along it to his special train, snugly concealed here from city crowds during the post-war election visit to the capital ; but now the platform is demolished and the Balerno branch line which, with a service of diesel cars, might almost have rivalled the Forth Bridge run in popularity awaits the arrival of some more enterprising proprietor than a railway company whose main concern seems to be how quickly it can close down its entire system.

The great paper-mill at Balerno, like its companion a mile or two down river at Kinleith, is a fairly close rival to the mills on the North Esk, if not so large. All the Midlothian mills are makers of fine papers, and the esparto grass which is perhaps the principal raw material can be seen almost any morning in big, dingy bales stacked on lorries roaring along the Lanark Road. Granton indeed is the chief British port for the import of this Spanish crop. Both the Balerno and the Kinleith mills proclaim their presences by lofty brick chimneys which tower above the little winding valley, structures so high that they could almost serve as landmarks for ships in the Firth ten miles away ; but in their beginnings those mills crouched close by the stream-side, drawing their power from the mill-lades as they drew the water for the processes of manufacture. Paper-milling on the Water of Leith seems to go back to the seventeenth century at least, and the Balerno mill dates from the eighteenth. The poisonous effluents which the mills used to discharge into the stream are no longer disposed of in this way, so that the brown pools now shelter a few small trout, and an occasional heron or even a kingfisher can be seen in the shadows of the overhanging trees.

Balerno village was at one time the focus of quite a number of moderate-sized mansions set in pleasant parklands. Bavelaw Castle up on the hill overlooking Threipmuir Reservoir has been a simple piece of seventeenth-century vernacular, the lands being granted by the King in 1628 to Laurence Scott of Harperrig, an advocate. Cockburn House nearby is another place of about the same period. Riccarton or Richardtown was rather earlier, and stood in a fine, wooded park ; but it has fallen a victim to the demolition-gangs which range so eagerly over Scotland, their motto apparently being : " There's an auld hoose—ca' it doon ! "

Then just in the shadow of the pretty gardens of Lymphoy, over-hanging the Water of Leith, is Lennox Tower, possibly having some connection with Darnley's father. Mary Queen of Scots herself is said to have liked this little castle as a hunting-lodge, and James VI's name and George Heriot's too have been associated with it. The great Montrose rested briefly at Lymphoy. Curriehill, just over the ridge on the side of the river opposite to Lymphoy, had a long association with the Bench, matching the associations which R. L. Stevenson attached to Hermiston, to the northward, but here again the housebreakers have been at work, and even the stately timber of the park has not been spared. These are not great homes, or famous ones, perhaps, but many another country would have prized them as gracious little adjuncts of its capital city. The Scots keep their pride for St. Andrew's night and without a fight surrender a countryside like this to invasion of the speculative builder.

This fate threatens too the village of Currie. Currie has maintained its rural character remarkably, considering it lies within six miles of the centre of Edinburgh. The village itself had no particular beauties, but there is a lovely old brig across the Water of Leith, leading to a simple but pleasing old church rising on the site of a pre-Reformation place of worship. A monument in the kirkyard, as well as the silver Communion cups, one of which dates from the last years of the sixteenth century, carry the name of Matthew Lichton or Leighton, nephew of the great Arch-bishop Leighton and himself distinguished as a curate of the parish under the Episcopalian régime and one who did not lose his living when Presbyterianism returned, since he stood so high in the affections of his parishioners. Close to the kirk is the delightful manse, snug within its walled garden. It has had a long series of worthy tenants, ranging from one who pursued the study of gun-barrels, much as a more celebrated Aberdeenshire minister occupied himself with gun-locks, to the late incumbent the Rev. David Stewart, whose fund of droll tales, often at his own expense, was known from one end of Scotland to the other. Not far from the manse is the Poet's Glen, the poet in question being a weaver who rhymed while he worked, in the Tannahill tradition.

Apart from the great Kinleith paper-mill, which fills the valley below Currie, industry has not spoiled the course of the water hereabouts. Every bend has its mill-lade, relic of times when the Water of Leith literally worked its way down to the sea, but most of the many mills have crumbled into ruin. Two of the most unusual were the snuff-mills above and below Juniper Green, mills which ceased to grind out their quaint product only in recent years. I remember them well as a boy. The upper one leaned towards the slow, brown water with a medieval sag, its diamond-paned windows obscured by the pinkish-brown dust, which clung to the very cobwebs that hung from the rafters inside. More than one box of its snuff I have smuggled away to school. It was a picturesque mill, with its timber bridge across the water, and this once was the most-painted corner of the valley. Nearby is a farmlet called Happy Family, formerly noted for its herd of tiny ponies which a generation ago were much in demand for drawing the coach of Cinderella in Edinburgh pantomimes. The Happy Family and the erstwhile snuff-mill are on the City Boundary of Edinburgh, but in this instance I propose to trespass and to cross the boundary, for the Pentlands are a province in themselves which no town and county councils can divide up into lots, whatever they may presume to do on paper.

Proceeding down the Water of Leith, the next village in succession to Currie has the lyrical name of Juniper Green. I have the less scruple in including it within the county because even yet some of its older inhabitants insist on completing their letter-headings with "Midlothian" instead of the "Edinburgh" which no doubt the post office deems correct; and although the village was never as attractive as its name it has managed to cling to a certain rural air in spite of the efforts made to extinguish its character by covering its cornfields with council houses and the bungalows of speculators. As with Currie, it is the river which has saved it. The desecrators can destroy the Muir Wood, but it is less easy to divert a river or to propose a really practical piece of desecration in the narrow confines of a glen. Some of the older houses in the village have a gaunt and strained look which I do not remember them to have had thirty years ago. The Gowanlea of David Masson, which has looked across at the Carlyles going visiting, and at Chalmers and Jeffrey, and maybe

Cairnpapple Hill, a Bronze Age burial-place

Torphichen Preceptory, originally the chief seat of the Hospitallers of St. John

at historical figures of far older times, has now become a mere number in the Lanark Road. Woodhall House, on the opposite side of the water, was a home of the Foulises. Perhaps its greatest claim to fame, however, is that its library was for a time the repository of the Bannatyne Manuscript, now in the National Library of Scotland—one of the principal collections of medieval Scots verse, brought together by George Bannatyne in the sixteenth century, whose daughter Janet married into the Foulis family and took the precious papers with her. To the north of the village again is a seventeenth-century mansion now called Baberton House, but in the old days known as Kilbaberton. Sir James Murray, the King's architect received a grant of the lands from Jamie the Saxt in 1612. His son, James Murray, Royal Master of Works, built the house about 1623, and his initials and his wife's are carved in various places. Baberton stands in a fine, wooded park, preserved from the invading housing estates by the existence of one of the best golf courses within the bounds of Edinburgh, the first few holes of which skirt the Baberton policies. There are some fine interiors in the house, which for a time was the home of the exiled King of France, Charles X. The presence of these worthy old houses does much to lend Juniper Green its air of county rather than town.

The next and last of the Pentland villages which cling to the Water of Leith is Colinton. Colinton has long been swallowed up by the city and can hardly be described as rural, even in the degree in which Juniper Green remains rural. Its many Edwardian villas, some of them Old English, more of them good, solid Scots rather in the Lorimer manner, are set in fine gardens and well hedged-about with amenities which keep encroachments comfortably at bay ; but these are essentially suburban dwellings, in the best and most exclusive sense, of course. Yet the real Colinton is the village by the river, on a particularly choice beat of the river. The valley widens here to an amphitheatre where the sun's warmth collects on a summer evening and the Water of Leith winds through it on the shady side, overhung with hanging woods which blaze with colour in the autumn. The village street winds down to meet it with a disregard for bends and gradients unusual even in such a B-class road, and doubles back upon itself at a lower level towards the cool shade of the Dell. Here, in an aroma of water-weeds with a perpetual hint of autumn in it and memories of burning leaves, the water makes a great bend under the over-hanging branches of trees climbing steeply towards the light, and within the bend lie the parish kirk of Colinton, and the kirkyard, and the manse. This is the focal point of Old Colinton. Clattering down the Kirk Brae and up through the village went the troops of Monk and, a little later, the little Covenanting army going to its tryst with fate at Rullion Green. The history of Colinton, however, is more interesting than stirring. Even in the days of the coach and the noddy the village held escape from care for many of the well-to-do citizens of Edinburgh, and a sort of aura of the law at ease hangs like a picturesque if somewhat chilly autumn mist among the oaks and beeches. Dr. Murray, who wrote the annals of the place more than a century ago, calls it the Tusculum of Edinburgh. Lord Cockburn, who occupied Bonaly Tower up on the Pentland slopes overlooking the village referred to it as a paradise which he would never leave unless expelled by an avenging angel. At least two of the original Senators of the College of Justice were neighbours here, one of them, Sir James Foulis, of the oldest family in the parish. But it has been a stronghold of the professions in general, a kind of rural and secluded extension of Heriot Row and Great King Street and Moray Place and all those dignified Edinburgh homes with their discreet brass plates. Almost the only stamp of commerce on the place is the tomb in the kirk of James Gillespie, founder of the school of that name, who made his money from the snuff which the Water of Leith ground out in such quantity. Spylaw House where he dwelt in all the pride of a self-made man is now in the public park, spanned by the main road-bridge and flanked by the railway. This tobacconist from the High Street was one of the worthiest men who found peace in Colinton, but in his day he had to suffer many a jibe, such as Henry Erskine's remark when he saw Gillespie in his first coach :

> Wha wad ha' thocht it
> That noses had bocht it ?

Colinton has perhaps always been marked by a certain professional class-superiority. In my earliest memories of it lingers a background impression of very proper at-homes and dinner-parties matching precisely the Edwardian houses with their well-tended tennis-lawns and summer-houses and herbaceous borders, their odour of lilies in conservatories, their discreet tinkling of tea-cups.

Belonging intimately and yet again belonging not at all with this is the Colinton of Robert Louis Stevenson. It has two centres. The first of these is the kirk and manse, where Stevenson's grandfather, the Rev. Lewis Balfour, was minister. The setting of these buildings is beautiful, and it is the sort of shadowed and dolorous beauty which would make a deep impression on the mind of an imaginative child. If Colinton manse had been otherwise placed than it is the work of R. L. S. might have been quite other than it is. The yews and the cypresses of that kirkyard early sunk in twilight by the dominating wooded height above, the incessant hoot of the owls in the enfolding trees and the stormy clamour of the branches on winter nights, the murmur of the water over the shallows whether in the heat of a summer's day or with the moonlight stealing in blue through a bedroom window : those are the very stuff of the spunkies and goblins, the nameless, dark deeds and the nocturnal escapes that make up one side of Stevenson's writing. The restless quest for far places may have had its birth here too, for this woody hollow is confining and sometimes stifling, and the river's coming into it from the unseen hills and its escape through the Dell towards the faraway sea rouse curiosity in what lies round the bend and over the horizon. Lewis Balfour himself probably had an immense influence on his small grandson. To one with Bohemian ways, he was a remote and rather austere figure in after-life, and his reiterated denunciations of the consumption of " ardent spirits " in the parish in his contribution to the *Statistical Account* of 1839 may even have diverted Stevenson ; but he was a scholar, with a sense of style and deep preoccupation with the life and lore of his parish, and the part played by the Balfours of Pilrig in Stevenson's novels is in itself a mark of the impact of the minister of Colinton. There was indeed a strong aura of scholarship on the manse. The incumbent prior to Balfour was the Rev. John Fleming, a broad-clothed and broad-minded

philosopher who left his books to the parish and his money to
aid chairs of political economy in Edinburgh and Glasgow. The
minister before him was John Walker, a botanist so distinguished
that he was made first occupant of the Chair of Natural History
in Edinburgh. He turned the manse garden at Colinton into
something like a botanic garden, and so precise was he sartorially
that Colinton society suspected his butterfly-net to be a device
for dressing his wig. John Walker contributed the account of the
parish of "Collington" to the first *Statistical Account*. The
author had a great deal more to say than Sir John Sinclair could
find room for, and the information not included was published in
London in 1812 as a small volume, which contains much interesting botanical and agricultural information about the state of
the parish at the end of the eighteenth century.

The second centre of Stevenson's Lothian was probably an
even more important one in the feeding of the first fires of his
genius. It is the hamlet of Swanston, within the parish of
Colinton but high above the village on the slopes of Caerketton,
the most easterly spur of those "hills of home" which for
Stevenson symbolised that country from which health drove
him into bitterly unwilling exile. That Swanston should ever
have come to overlook a city public park could only horrify
the lonely figure who so often used to play truant from more
crowded places in its cleughs and woods—it is within sound now
of more than the hum of bees and the far-off barking of John
Todd's collie. Still, Swanston in itself is not so changed that it is
difficult to shed the years, the hundred years, and think back to a
day when Stevenson drew from the old stones and the shade of
the beeches and the blink of the flowers in the garden in July
that essence of the place which he gave us back in honeyed
descriptions to which odours still cling with a power like withered
rose-leaves in a bowl to recreate what is gone. Stevenson is
remembered as a master of English rather than of the Scots
vernacular, but his memories of Colinton parish persuaded him
into giving us some of the most telling Scots verse of modern
times. His "stench auld farrant firs" at Swanston are as deft
a word-sketch as could be, and his description of the walk down
hill to church is a brilliant mingling of word-picture with mis-
chievous commentary—

But hark ! the bells frae nearer clang ;
To rowst the slaw their sides they bang ;
An' see ! black coats a'ready thrang
    The green kirkyaird.
And at the yett the chestnuts spang
    That brocht the laird.

Stevenson in all probability absorbed at Swanston much of his
knowledge of the Scots tongue. It was the only country place
where his roots were deep enough to develop that convincing,
earthy flavour in his verse. And probably a great deal more than
his mastery of Scots can be traced back to the Swanston days.
In *Virginibus Puerisque* he writes " The age that we have reached,
as the phrase goes, we but hold with an outpost, and still keep
open our communications with the extreme rear and first beginnings of the march. There is our true base ; that is not only
the beginning, but the perennial spring of our faculties . . . "
Swanston was certainly the perennial spring of Stevenson's
faculties. " I think I owe my taste for that hillside business rather
to the art and interest of John Todd. He it was that made it live
for me . . ." And he goes on nostalgically to paint his memory of
the Caerketton slopes—the massing sheep on the snowy expanse,
yellow upon white, the air " that took you by the throat," the
howl of the wind on the moorland, and above all the masterful
figure of the shepherd, " his great voice taking hold upon the
hills."

Strangely, the great voice that has taken hold upon the hills is
no longer John Todd's, but the voice of the wistful, rather sickly
lad who only sat and watched. And the echoes of it sound not
only on the hills, but down all the wooded cleughs into every
nook and dell of the Water of Leith itself. " That dirty Water of
Leith," as he called it. Every bend and eddy of it is remembered.
There are the weirs, where the water lies " deep and darkling,"
receiving the contents of the mill-lades, which set the " curded
froth of many other mills solemnly steering to and fro upon the
surface." And in the dark, hanging woods he recalls " the smell
of water rising from all around, with an added tang of paper-
mills, the sound of water everywhere, and the sound of mills
—the wheel and the dam singing their alternate strain ; the birds

on every bush and from every corner of the overhanging woods pealing out their notes until the air throbbed with them." Even in his day Stevenson realised that " change, and the masons, and the pruning-knife, have been busy," and that he could not hope to see it all again as it was when he was small. Happily, the heart of it all has not changed greatly yet. If we, as Stevenson himself put it, " choose the season," it would be hard among the yews of that water-encompassed kirkyard to believe that the spare, stooping form of Tusitala does not still tread the turf sometimes.

CHAPTER SIX

The Oil Belt

BETWEEN THE slopes of the Pentlands and the shores of the Firth lies a plain with a curious topography. From any vantage point such as the Kaimes Hill or the ridge of Currie, the low ground to the northward is seen to be scattered with red hills, flat-topped and oddly uniform in type, although not in size. In the light of a westering sun some of the hills appear quite massive and suggest the results of primeval eruptions. In the candid morning light the hills can be seen for what they are, colossal shale bings ; but even face to face the older and larger of the bings have acquired a certain dignity and impressiveness, and as the bushes and young trees and the drifts of willowherb climb their lower slopes and help to integrate them with the country-side they cease to be quite the insult to nature which they no doubt once were, and become not much more objectionable than some volcanic phenomenon such as the vanished Pink Terraces of New Zealand. The red of them is a russet brick-colour which weathers well. The rawness has gone from most of them. They are the Scottish equivalent of the oil-derricks of Texas and the Caucasus and Iraq ; yet they are a very different sort of symbol, for the crowding, ramshackle gushers speak of easy wealth where the slow accumulations of those red hills of waste tell of a long grim fight to win the riches from the earth.

The material in those heaps has, of course, all come from deep underground. When first mined, it has quite a different form and consistency, but the spent shale takes the form of compressed leaves or layers of material rather like a favourite cake of my schooldays known, if I remember rightly, as a vanilla sandwich. The laminations are significant. They point to a constant succession of deposits, regular and with only a brief interval between, and the theory is that each layer represents a tidal precipitation. The bulk of each precipitation was composed of fine, silted mud—the inorganic material which now goes to make up those waste heaps; but suspended in the mud was a percentage of animal and plant residue, and this is the stuff from which the oils and other products are obtained. It will be seen that the oil shales are near cousins to the coal measures, which are the compressed remains of primeval forests. The broad difference is that the oil shales were laid down in water, and in a state of fine precipitate. If final proof were needed it lies in the fossilised remains of fish and other forms of submarine life which occur in great numbers in the oil shales, finny ghosts scattered throughout the black Pumpherston shales. The frilly impressions of ferns and other land plants may be explained as the scourings of river banks. It would seem, then, that this strip of the Lothians which I have called the oil belt was once a tidal lagoon of about 300 square miles in extent, into which rivers poured their waters. Fossilised branches and seeds indicate that the land around was heavily forested with conifers, and portions of the trunk of one of the enormous trees were at one time dug up and exhibited in Edinburgh.

The shales are mined, however, as I have already mentioned, at great depths. How do the remains of the tidal lagoon come to be thousands of feet beneath the Lothian fields? H. M. Cadell of Grange, in his *The Story of the Forth*, drew a clear picture of what came about. The lagoon became the home of enormous numbers of crustaceans, whose shells built up over the bed of the lagoon into a layer of limestone—the well-known Burdiehouse limestone—sometimes as much as 30 feet thick. Another period of shale deposition seems to have followed; then came successions of sandstone, shales and coal, the last the result of an overgrowth of the lagoon by forest. Then follows a thick layer of the rock known as Houston Marl, which appears to be a build-up of volcanic ash. If this marl is in fact volcanic a period of fierce eruptive activity must have destroyed the forest-covered lagoon. Life overspread the resultant wilderness again, leaving more coal-beds. The land sank and the sea intervened for a time. When it receded, an age of fetid swamps and forests followed, inhabited by carnivorous monsters which have left their teeth in the huge coal-measures which resulted. The background to this sinister swamp-life of the Carboniferous Limestone era was renewed volcanic activity, and this in a sense brings us to the surface of the West Lothian countryside, for the most prominent features, indeed the only massive natural features, are the crests of the lava streams which survive in the Bathgate and Linlithgow hills.

The "oil towns" are scattered over an area of about 75 square miles. They are marked usually by the presence of the great red bings, which can rise from nothing to a height of 200 feet and more in less than twenty years. Many of the towns, of course, date from long before the "oil boom." West Calder, for example, was a century ago a rural community with only a little coal and ironstone mining in the vicinity, and its products were mainly cattle, butter and cheese " of excellent quality," to quote the *Statistical Account*. To-day, instead of shrinking, like most rural communities, it is expanding, and its amenities have not been diminished by a colony of Swedish timber houses to the east of it, into which—for a wonder, in Scotland !—the road-side trees have been integrated to form a pleasant avenue of approach. The expansion is due in part at least to the big new shale-pit to the north. This is the latest of the Lothian shale-pits, dating only from the Second World War. A visit to it opens wide a door upon an industry which, in spite of its importance is known hardly at all even in the Lothians, and probably few of those who plough the quiet fields hereabouts realise that deep below these green copses and flowering hedges sounding with nothing louder than a chaffinch or a wood-pigeon men are labouring in a labyrinth of tunnels to maintain the roar of traffic in the streets of Edinburgh and Glasgow.

The Westwood oil works is at first sight not unlike a coal pit —a modern coal pit, with flower beds in front of the administra-tive offices, and the buildings constructed neatly of a pleasant pinkish brick which is a by-product of the industry. Pit-headgear and shaft are also in the coal-mining tradition. The drop to the pit-bottom is 700 feet. This too resembles the bottom of a coal pit, but one notices at once the greater height of the tunnels in the shale mine, for the shale seams here are much thicker than the average coal seam. A long, straight gradient leads down towards one of the working "faces," and in one or two of the man-holes by the way the beam of the torch picks out the sight, rather unusual in a shale pit, of natural oil oozing blackly from a crack in the shale, like a smear of treacle. At the face, however, there is nothing but a cavern of what seems to be black, splintered rock, dry but for a slight condensation from the humid air-stream. Close inspection shows the laminations in the shale, although their tidal origin appears to be even farther off than the 19 million years which some ingenious calculator has set as the age of these shales. The remains of drill-holes for the ex-plosive charges can be detected all over the face. It is interesting to find that old-fashioned gunpowder is still the charge used, the reason being that a more violent explosive would shatter the shale into fragments too small to be suitable for the retorts, while in a shale mine the danger of gases being ignited by the flame is not great.

The shale comes to the surface in sizeable pieces, averaging a few pounds in weight. In the light of day it looks an even less likely material than it does in the depths of the mine, and it has to be converted into crude oil before it attains the state in which it is found in the world's great oilfields. This second stage, of conversion, is symbolised at Westwood by the huge retorts. To make the production of shale oil economically possible at all, the retorting stage must be highly efficient, especially where the deposits of shale are, as in West Lothian, not enormous. Great heat is the primary element in the conversion process. It must be generated and maintained with the minimum of expense. A new process was therefore devised in which some of the carbon in the shale itself was utilised to provide the heat, so that the material to be retorted virtually provides its own fuel. The great vertical retorts, dramatic structures even in the broad light of day, are fed at the top with the raw material by means of a belt con-veyor, and the spent shale is discharged at the bottom and cooled off by means of water sprays ; but the very steam generated by the spent shale is injected back into the retort to help distribute the heat, among other things ; and even the spent gases are sucked out into waste-heat boilers to produce further supplies of steam. This highly concentrated process goes on in no fewer than 104 retorts, which between them can consume more than a thousand tons of crushed shale every day. The crude oil is produced in the form of oil vapour, which has to be washed and condensed. The other products are ammonia liquor, crude spirit, and permanent gas. The gas goes back into the retorts for heating. The ammonia is treated with sulphuric acid to form sulphate of ammonia in a crystallised form suitable for use as an agricultural stimulant, and the sulphate is automatically weighed into bags and sewn up. The spirit, like the oil, proceeds to the refinery. These new and more economical processes have made their mark on the landscape already, for the fully utilised spent shale which piles up in the newer bings is much darker in colour than the rather picturesque red material of former times.

The mining side of the West Lothian industry is closely integrated with the refining, as a single day's scrutiny shows clearly; but it is equally clear that the mines have their own problems, for the refinery can and does deal with crude oil no matter what its source and therefore is not threatened by foreign sources of production to the same extent. The threat to the shale-oil industry is very real. Mine after mine has closed down. Bing after bing is going back to nature, perhaps to the benefit of the landscape but not to the advantage of the population. Shale-mining in West Lothian is vulnerable because it cannot compete economically with the natural crude-oil fields abroad, even allowing for shipping costs; and it is on too small a scale to compete in the future with the gigantic shale-oil deposits of America, which have as yet hardly been tapped. The chief virtue of the Lothian product is that it is a home product, and therefore an asset in times of difficulty. Diesel and spirit made from Lothian oil sell at the same prices as imported fuels, and the only advantage which the home product carries is that the equivalent of the import tax is added to the company's takings, a modest subsidy much needed in the struggle to survive. Lothian shales do not supply in themselves fuel for any portion of our transport, but blended with a proportion of diesel refined from oil imported from England, Scottish diesel can be said to fuel the public transport of Edinburgh and Glasgow. How long it may go on doing this is doubtful. Not only has the Scottish industry imports to contend with, but it has to face the competition of other industries in Scotland. Coal mining in particular is a rival in the labour market, for it offers better wages, and the shale miner can adapt himself easily to the closely similar technique of winning coal. The expanding coalfields of the neighbouring Lothians, still more the developing fields of Fife on the opposite shore of the Firth, are always to some extent a magnet for the shale miner.

The refining centre of the oil industry is the village of Pumpherston, lying about midway between Uphall and Midcalder. Village is perhaps hardly the word for it, if village implies something rural. Instead of farm-steadings surrounded by stacks, Pumpherston has a huddle of factories and sidings surrounded by eroded old shale bings ; and instead of manor-house there is the old mansion of Middleton Hall, a mile or two away, off the new Glasgow road, serving as administrative headquarters of the industry. But this enormous refinery has certain epic qualities of its own. The old bings about it date from 1883 onwards, when the works was erected to retort locally mined shale. They make a kind of Grand Canyon background to the tall chimneys and to the intricate maze of pipes which is the arterial system of this production plant. Closer inspection of the heart of the plant reveals a black oiliness on the pipes and on the very puddles in the bricked roadways, significant of the changes which have been wrought in the naturally dry and rather dusty shale. There is, too, a faintly sinister odour of gas in the air, although employees of the refinery assure me they are unaware of it.

The crude oil comes to the refinery in rail tank wagons and in tanker lorries, which discharge their somewhat revolting-looking contents into troughs in the ground. The crude oil is refined in the first instance by distillation and split into various " fractions " in a great multi-staged fractionation tower. The products are a wax-free oil, a wax-bearing oil, a small proportion of crude spirit, and a residue which gives a fine coke of low ash content—a chunky, clean-looking fuel which is hard to obtain in the ordinary market. The wax-bearing " cut " has to be rid of its crude wax, and this is achieved by blending it with wax-free oil and running the mixture through an enormous refrigerating system in the pipes of which scrapers revolve to remove the wax. The chill of the refrigeration plant is a grim contrast to the heat of the neighbouring furnaces with their gases flaming from nozzles into incandescent brick chambers. The de-waxed oil and wax-free oil form the main content of the crude diesel output of the refinery, which is treated and re-distilled to produce diesel fuel.

Motor spirit is obtained from the lightest portion of the crude oil distillation, crude naphtha, and spirit from the cracking of heavy oil, a blend which is treated chemically and distilled and purified, and finally blended with some high-octane spirit to comply with the specification.

The by-products of the shale-oil industry are in some ways more interesting to the layman than the main products. One of the most important is the wax which is removed from the oil. A considerable space in the Pumpherston works is devoted to the purifying and preparation of this wax. The crude wax from the filter presses contains a fair percentage of oil, which renders it dark in colour and unstable. Oil is removed by a sweating process. First, oil comes out of the sweaters, then waxes of higher and higher melting-points ; then, to decolour it, the molten wax is passed through great vertical cylinders containing Fuller's earth, the wax passing into trays where it sets hard in thick, white slabs, ready for the market. Candles are still made from it at Broxburn, but the demand for candles is of course not what it was—Lothian candle-wax, they say, was to be found in wayside shrines all over Russia until the fall of Rasputin !—and the wax now goes in the main to make grease-proof packings, water-proofed materials, and insulators for the electrical industry. It is hard to say which is in greater contrast to the rugged shale in the darkness of the pit-bottom : the smooth white wax lying in neat piles in the packing-shed, or the clear motor spirit. Other products of Pumpherston are quantities of ammonium sulphate for agriculture, caustic soda used in the refining process, a pleasant, dark strawberry-coloured building brick made from the spent shales, the plant having the considerable output of 6000 bricks per hour. To these has now been added synthetic detergent, produced in two forms, an amber-coloured liquid and a paste. It is those by-products of the shale oil which have kept the Lothian industry in being in the face of overwhelming competition, and there are few monuments more significant of the fighting qualities of Scottish industry than the shale bings of West Lothian.

Shale oil is, however, a brief episode in Scotland's industrial history. It spans only about a hundred years. The man who presided over its beginning was John Young, dubbed " Paraffin Young " by his friend, Dr. Livingstone. Like so many pioneer technologists, Young's career lay at first along a very different path. He was a Glasgow cabinet-maker with such a liking for chemistry that he became in turn assistant to the professors of chemistry in Glasgow and in London. He first became interested in oil in a coal-pit in Derbyshire, where the appearance of a trickle of crude oil led him to conclude, correctly, that the oil was a distillation from the coal. In 1850 he took out a patent. Shortly after, he found a rich vein in what he took to be cannel coal at Torbanehill, near Bathgate ; but it was really an exceptionally rich oil shale—so rich, indeed, that it yielded 120 gallons of crude oil per ton, compared with the 35 to 40 of the richest oil shales worked to-day. The Torbanehill deposit became exhausted in a matter of a dozen years, and when Young's patent expired a year or two later the industry expanded so rapidly on less-rich seams that in 1871 there were 51 small paraffin works with a crude oil production of 25 million gallons.

The obtrusive shale bings seem at first sight to proclaim that the mineral wealth of West Lothian depends principally on oil and its by-products. They obscure the more prosaic coal pit-heads. The basic product, however, is coal, not oil. It is not oil but coal which has the future here. The Torbanehill cannel is exhausted, but the names of Armadale and Blackburn and Addiewell, to say nothing of Bathgate and Torphichen, are synonymous with coal, and even in the gently rural lanes which wander with an English aimlessness about some of these parishes one meets with incongruous parties of miners with faces paled and grimed and lamps glinting dully in the morning sun. There are something like 200 million tons of coal reserves : not a very large figure by East Lothian or Fife standards, but enough to insure work for a generation or two. Fear that the reserves of coal would be worked out has been endemic in West Lothian for something like four hundred years, and an Act of the reign of Mary Queen of Scots banned its export on this ground.

On the southern fringe of the mining belt is a long strip of rural country stretching from the bounds of Edinburgh itself south-westwards along the edge of the Pentlands. It is scarcely marked at all by industry, except where the shale hummocks of West Calder and Pumpherston dwarf the natural contours.

Even the bings, however, are dwarfed by the great crag-and-tail scarp of the Kaimes and Dalmahoy hills, which command the whole of the West Lothian plain, and their stony summits are probably the stronghold of early man in this region, as Traprain was at the other end of the Lothians. No treasure has been dug up here. The only relics are some fragments of pottery, a piece of a bronze ring and a *denarius* of the reign of Severus which came out of a rabbit hole. But both hilltops have had extensive fortifications, now no more than tumbled boulders. Kaimes must have had a considerable settlement, for among the stones and hill-grass can be traced the marks of two or three dozen hut-circles, while on the verge of the north scarp is a well which must have allowed defenders of this fort to hold out for indefinite periods. The enclosed area is as much as ten acres. The green fields and woods which now stretch out at the scarp's foot no doubt were in the days when the early Britons lived here in bogs and bush country. Now they comprise the vale of the Almond Water, which for most of its length is the boundary between Mid and West Lothian. The Almond and the burns that run into it in its upper reaches rise in that great, bleak expanse of heathland which embraces the moors of Shotts and Polkemmet and Fauldhouse, rolling country from 600 to 800 feet above sea-level, a mist-damped, cloud-dappled brown grassland country of sheep and whaups which hides considerable riches in coal and ironstone; but on its right bank from Blackburn down the river flanks as pretty agricultural land as there is in Lothian.

This might be called the country of the Calders. The three Calders—West, Mid and East—are the spine of it, at one time no doubt a chain of pleasant little villages. Over the past century, West Calder has changed, but of that I have said something earlier in this chapter. It is enough to add that in the thirty years between 1850 and 1880 the population grew from 2000 to nearly 8000. West Calder itself has no special natural features, but the parish reaches out to the largest loch in Midlothian, Cobbinshaw reservoir, a well-stocked stretch of water set in rather inhospitable surroundings. " Shaw," of course, signifies a forest, and it seems there was once a forest here of the name of Colinshaw ; but the trees fell and rotted, and the ground became a bog, and in 1822 the water was dammed up to form a supply cistern for the Union Canal. About the same time extensive drainage schemes transformed the whole of this upland. None did more to bring this about than the Laird of Crosswoodhill, a nearby farm, who wrote an absorbing and valuable treatise on the drainage of peat-mosses, based on his own practice. For the layman, the treatise is a graphic record of the herculean efforts of Lothian landowners, which turned some of the worst farming land in the world into some of the best. One-third of Crosswoodhill's land was deep peat bog when he took it over, and even on the rest the crops rarely ripened and the sheep sickened of " the rot "; but he " dug to the bottom of every spring and quacking (*sic*) bog " and constructed much more than a hundred miles of drains, built dry-stone dykes, planted shelterbelts of spruce and fir and completed his improvements with dressings of compost which make his treatise read like the work of a modern disciple of organic farming. Like so many of the enlightened Scots landowners of that golden age, he was a bit of a scholar. He knew the Linnæan nomenclature even of the bog-plants which he was trying to get rid of, and he preserved with care the Roman silver coins which his farm-servants dug up when making the drains, noting the names of the emperors on them and speculating about the legionaries who dropped them, and at the same time he experimented with composts and speculated on the nature of lime and its chemistry with the help of Pliny and Vitruvius.

The lower ground of the Calder country must always have been well-wooded, for the name seems to originate in some version of the Gaelic for " the wood by the water." The Almond and its tributaries wind gently by little woods in a shallow vale, once the manor of Calder-Comitis, or Earl's Calder, as it belonged to the Thanes or Earls of Fife. This is, on the whole, a backwater of history. There are some fine mansions, but none is linked with specially stirring events. Calder House, to the west of Midcalder, seat of the Sandilands family which has been the possessor of the Calder lands since the fourteenth century, has a link with John Knox, but the present house goes back no further than the seventeenth century. Linhouse, on the Linhouse Water, which enters the Almond at Midcalder, dates in part from 1589. Midcalder itself is a pleasant enough village without having claim to any particular amenities, but its late-Gothic parish kirk is

The gateway of Linlithgow Palace

rather beautiful, its first rector having been a member of the Sandilands family just before the Reformation. The best features of the kirk are external ones, but there is a carved pew-back, dated 1595, with the arms of the Sandilands and a line from the 23rd Psalm. The Reformation intervened before the church could be completed, but full instructions were left by Master Peter Sandilands, the rector, and some of the detail, for example on the pinnacles, is quite elaborate. The kirk is well bowered in trees against the west winds roaring in across the Shotts moors, and in their shelter lie some interesting gravestones, one at least dating from the first half of the seventeenth century. It is worth recording that the second minister of Calder, the Rev. John Spottiswoode, was the representative sent by the General Assembly in 1566 to "testify their gladness" to the Queen on the birth of the prince who was to be James VI. She listened with "reverent attention" while he called down the blessing of God upon the child, but his plea for a baptism according to the rites of the Reformed Kirk found no response. His son, of the same name, followed him in the kirk of Calder; but in the disputes between Kirk and Crown he took the King's side, and he ended up as that Archbishop Spottiswoode who placed the crown on Charles I's head at Holyrood in 1625.

The third and easternmost of the Calders is almost a continuation of Midcalder, but it lacks Midcalder's happy situation at the junction of two tributaries with the Almond Water, and it lacks too the road junctions which give interest to the layout of the neighbour village. It is no mere extension of Midcalder, however. Its history is distinct. In the old documents it is called Calder Clere, as opposed to Calder Comitis, as it was granted to one Randolph de Clere by Malcolm IV. But nothing is left of its past except the old parish church, ruinous and with "the roof already decayit" as early as 1627. It now comes within the parish of Kirknewton, the name-village of which is a hamlet on the road to nowhere in particular. Kirknewton could easily be a pretty village, but the art of growing old gracefully is uncommon in this part of the Lothians, in spite of an abundance of good building freestone, lime and sand. It may be the soil is too heavy and demands too much grim labour to encourage the lighter country crafts and pursuits, but one cannot help contrasting the austerity

The House of the Binns; a view of the dining-room

of the Calder country with some of the villages of Dumfries-shire, East Fife or the south coast of Sutherland, where charming, well-kept cottages are set off by gardens riotous with old-fashioned flowers. Yet the village has sheltered as many men of liberal culture as most within a morning's trot of the Parliament House in Edinburgh. In the kirkyard lies William Cullen, one of the greatest among the many great teachers of medicine of the Edinburgh School, although perhaps his most imperishable memorial is to be sought among the wild flowers which he scattered as seed on his estate of Ormiston Hill, in his botanising zeal. Near him lies his son Robert, described on his monument as "an eminent judge, an elegant scholar, and an accomplished gentleman." The Rev. Alexander Bryce, minister of the parish from 1745 to 1786, combined with his pastoral duties a disting-uished reputation as geometrician and geographer. Another distinguished judge was Allan Maconochie of Meadowbank, a founder of the Speculative Society, that exclusive body, in although not of the University of Edinburgh, whose debates by candlelight have heard such speakers as Brougham, Francis Horner, Lord John Russell, and Lord Jeffrey.

East of the Calders is a rural enclave contained by the Almond Water, the foothills of the Pentlands and the western bounds of Edinburgh. Edinburgh itself probably knows little about this unspoilt territory almost within sound of the city traffic. Four trunk roads flank or strike through it. At night, points of light can be seen busily skimming along them, often almost touching, like glowing drops of water chasing one another down a sloping telegraph wire, and at all times the hum of them spreads across the quiet of the fields to farms half hid in their copses ; but by a fortunate chance the lateral roads cross-linking the trunks, although there is a maze of them, are rather wayward and a little baffling, and there is not much temptation for motorists, still less for lorries or motor-buses, to leave the main roads. After dark, I myself have the greatest difficulty in finding my way due south across this enclave from South Queensferry to my home. It involves nearly as much tacking as sailing into the teeth of a gale, and a wrong turning will almost certainly in the end lead one to some midden with inky moat, the sinister waters of which loom black in the glare of the headlights. In broad daylight, on the other hand, it is rather reassuring to be able to get lost among rambling lanes and to know that the stark "planning" of the housing estate has not yet got this far.

There is neither village of great note nor are there many stately mansions to draw strangers into the district. Its attraction is the attraction of good land well maintained over the centuries in its fertility, so that there is a bloom on the fields and parks and a well-bigged look about the homes of the men and women who live and work there.

Ratho village, with its low whinstone houses, is a pleasant little place, if not so very old. Part of its single street used to be called the Lud Gate, or Lord's Gate, because it led to the church. The church, although much rebuilt, has a long history. It was dedicated to the Virgin Mary in the twelfth century, and a Norman doorway and one or two buttresses of slightly later date have survived, but the main portion of the building seems to have been put up in the seventeenth century, and there is a date 1683 over a doorway. In Ratho parish, too, is the recently burned-out shell of the extensive mansion of Hatton House. The gateway leading to it—the keystone is inscribed 1692—is on the north side of the Calder-Glasgow road, between Wilkieston and Burnwynd. The house is a somewhat unusual blend of renaissance features with the vernacular, for the most part built by Charles Maitland, afterwards third Earl of Lauderdale, in the later seventeenth century. Perhaps the most interesting room in it was the rather ornate little apartment in the south-east tower known as Lord Jeffrey's study, for the great Francis Jeffrey took Hatton for the summers of 1812 to 1815, possibly at the wish of Charlotte Wilkes, whom he brought back from America as his wife about that time. Many an article for the *Edinburgh Review* must have been penned in this room looking out upon the stately lawns of Hatton. By and large, Ratho cannot compare in literary fame with some of the other Lothian parishes, but it has produced a couple of poets who attained some celebrity in their own times. The first of these was Joseph Mitchell, born some time towards the end of the reign of Charles II. His father, a stone-mason, determined that Joseph should go into the ministry, and to that end somehow contrived to put him through the university; but he preferred the precarious career of letters and went to London, where he found his way into the company of many distinguished writers, among them Walpole. He made little from his craft, but he wrote some plays and published in 1724 two large volumes of verse, one poem being a plea to the King to restore his native village of Ratho to a former state of glory which seems to belong to his own imagination rather than to history—

> Of ancient Ratho, reared with cost and pain,
> How few and wretched monuments remain !

The other Ratho poet, William Wilkie, has been called the Scottish Homer on the strength of a piece of epic verse called the *Epigonaid*, based on the Fourth Book of the Iliad, but apart from this he was a man of considerable distinction. A descendant of the Wilkies of Ratho Byres, he was born in 1721 and subsequently became minister of Ratho, but in 1761 he was appointed to the Chair of Moral Philosophy at St. Andrews. His conversational powers seem to have rivalled Samuel Johnson's. Like Johnson, too, he must have been an odd personality. Because of his profound knowledge of agriculture he was called the potato minister, and he became notorious for the number of blankets which he demanded on his bed, twenty-four pairs being in his view " just enough."

A short distance eastwards along the road from Hatton is the seventeenth-century gate to Dalmahoy. The gate apart, this estate has nothing of great antiquity on it, except a stone with a cross carved on it, near the little chapel, a symbol dating from the early days of Christianity in Scotland. For many years now Dalmahoy park has been a golf course, perhaps the best fate that can befall a great estate on the fringe of urban expansion. Farther east along the road again is Hermiston village, more properly Long Hermiston, fortuitously famed as the location of Stevenson's posthumous novel, but now mocked by the nearness of the most uninspired housing area in the capital city : Sighthill, a concrete wilderness built on some of the best farming land in Scotland. Indeed, the flank of this blessedly rural corner of Midlothian has been turned completely by the advance of a city curiously insensitive to the need to marry town and country. The architectural gem of the district, Corstorphine Kirk, has now long been included within the city's bounds, and the parish of Corstorphine is now a ward of the city; but here again as in the case of the valley of the Water of Leith there is, I think, some justification for trespassing, as historically Corstorphine is linked with its small neighbour Gogar, to the west, not with the metropolis. The name is intriguing. In the Ragman's Roll (1296) it is written *Crostorphyn*, giving us Cross of Torphin. Who or what Torphin was is obscure, but it is possible Johnson is right in interpreting it as *Torr fionn*, or white hill. There is a hill of this name above Juniper Green. The village is now almost entirely swamped by the city, but the old church remains an oasis among the shops and cinemas, and there is still a certain countrified air about its surroundings, helped by some good trees dating back to the days when fields spread on all hands—which is not so very long ago, as even I can recall a short holiday spent at Corstorphine when I was a child, the means of access to it from the city being a horse-cab. The old collegiate church is a lovely building. It is a low, grey structure with massively tiled roof and a tower which has been compared with the Pope's triple tiara. Unlike so many of the little churches of Scotland, it has an interior which is not at all disappointing. There are some fine sedilia and tombs, notably the tombs of the Forresters, who founded the church early in the fifteenth century and were the leading family of the parish from the year 1376. Adam Forrester, a great merchant, became in succession Provost of Edinburgh, Sheriff of Lothian, and Keeper of the Great Seal of Scotland. Taken prisoner at the battle of Homildon Hill, he was subsequently presented to King Henry IV. The stone which covered his tomb is in the church. The Forresters continued to be closely associated with the parish until the end of the seventeenth century.

What is now the "county" half of the old parish of Corstorphine is the lands of Gogar, farming country west of the Gogar Burn, which flows into the Almond. The name of Gogar is ancient and is sprinkled liberally over the map: Gogar Bank, Over Gogar, Gogar Park, Gogar Mains, to say nothing of Gogar village itself. The estate of this name was given by Robert the Bruce to Alexander Seton. Its history is not particularly stirring, except for the brief chapter in which Leslie baffled Cromwell and eventually forced him to retreat towards Musselburgh, an engagement largely fought out by the artillery, which may be why the field where the fight took place used to be called The Flashes. One theory has it that this skirmish accounts for the abnormal number of stone coffins found on the Gogar lands, coffins formed from flagstones which may have come from the bed of the Almond nearby. But perhaps the most remarkable antiquity of this part of the county is daily missed by thousands of travellers on the Glasgow road just before they come to New-bridge, a mile or two west of the Gogar lands. It is a great circular cairn contained by a low modern wall of stone, the circle about a hundred feet across and the mound rising to upwards of ten feet at the centre. Without the modern wall the thing might scarcely attract attention, might pass for a mere natural hummock in a flat field ; but it is in fact a link with prehistory, and probably quite an important one. Three standing stones which survive may indicate that the cairn was at one time surrounded by a circle of such stones. The cairn is a barrow, possibly of the Early Bronze Age.

The farmlands from Ratho and Gogar westwards are as prosperous as they look. This does not apply to the neighbour-hood of the coal and shale mines, where the soil is poor over a clay bottom, and where moreover the constant subsidences have broken up the tile-drains, so that in some places drifts of rushes are threatening the pastures. Elsewhere things are very different. The farms are not so large, probably not nearly so large as the famous farms of East Lothian, but they do very well. There are excellent wheat-lands just west of Edinburgh, and the distribu-tion of rainfall is favourable for root-crops and hay. A good deal of dairying is done, but the farmers no longer make butter and " soor-dook " for marketing in the city. Sheep are not much seen until one gets up to the high ground farther west, but pigs have been steadily increasing in numbers on city swill, especially among the numerous small-holdings encouraged by the Depart-ment of Agriculture in this area. Many of the small-holdings also maintain poultry.

Kirkliston parish is divided between Mid and West Lothian, and the village of the name is just inside the West Lothian boundary, beside a bend of the Almond. Its amenities are not outstanding, and its houses are not of great age—a century and a half ago some of them, according to the *Statistical Account*, were "little better than Irish cabins." At first sight even the church is not a notable building, dominated by an austere western tower, without any great window and not improved by a little seventeenth-century belfry, a functional afterthought. The south doorway, then, is all the more of a surprise, with its clustered columns and rich Norman arch with deep-cut chevrons. The doorway has suffered badly in the six centuries of its existence, but it has been described as one of the finest fragments of late Transitional work in Scotland. Other fragments of Transitional elsewhere marry with the unadorned work of the seventeenth century and after, and there is a fine arch linking the tower with the church itself. A burial vault on the south side carries a motto which seems to accord with the austerity of the church: VIRTVTE. DECET. NON. SANGVINE. NITI—"Put your trust in virtue, not in ancestry." The initials suggest James Dalrymple of Stair. This is the burial place of the Dalrymples, the Earls of Stair, among them Elizabeth Dundas, wife of the first earl and original of Lucy Ashton in *The Bride of Lammermoor*.

The remainder of this chapter is concerned with the wedge of country contained by the Glasgow and Linlithgow roads, west of Kirkliston. It must be country as unknown as any in the Lothians, but it is well worth exploring. The tide of traffic bypasses it, flowing westwards from Edinburgh along the two big trunk roads, which diverge from one another rapidly until there is neither sight nor sound of either and the pace of life slows down to a rural ride. The roads that serve this piece of country are obviously ancient ones that do really serve it. They follow its contours in a lazy, bewildering, delightful way that will set the motorist wrenching his wheel around and wildly slamming his gears, but with every yard they offer reward to anyone willing to walk them.

From the two trunk roads, one would never guess that the country between is interesting. A skyline with a few trees and perhaps a farm-steading is all that is visible. The easternmost part, the part, that is, between Kirkliston and Broxburn, has been contorted by the unnatural upheavals of the shale bings. As I have said earlier, these are not altogether without a certain curious beauty when vegetation comes to knit them into the landscape, and evening light and imagination between them can invest them with a certain amount of drama ; but at close quarters they are alien and impossible. They dwarf the proper scale, overhang old cottages and threaten to change the course of streams. Climbing westwards, however, one finds suddenly that they are gone. There is nothing but hedgerows and little fields and copses and a rolling horizon. The road switchbacks and winds through little woods and ferny thickets, with now and then a boggy clearing or a scrap of heathland which might be on the fringe of the Highlands. Only a mile or two away there are prosaic enough Lowland villages—Ecclesmachan and the Ochiltrees—but they are not visible, and the illusion is complete when the snout of Binny Craig appears ahead. Binny Craig acquires a grandeur out of all proportion to its real size, for it thrusts up from a scarp against a great space of sky like some mountain pinnacle, and the crows wheeling about it might, if there were not so many of them, be ravens. The road goes through a farm-steading or two, its black surface for a few yards brown with dung and mire from the carts. Then suddenly, as one nears the top of a long hill the landscape becomes magnificently spacious and it would be hard to find a view as superb anywhere in the Lothians. Like Binny, now rather dwarfed behind, the Riccarton Hills ahead appear remote and rather splendid, with their skirt of pine-forest to the east, and southwards are the Bathgate Hills, looking like the edge of nowhere and successfully hiding from us the reek and chimneys of Bathgate town. A deserted-looking road winds off to the left. It skirts the eminence, and presently a neat notice proclaims this to be Cairnpapple Hill. The summit of this strange place has been beautifully laid out by the Ancient Monuments branch of the Ministry of Works. Although it is merely a grassy mound surrounded by a rampart the effect is monumental. Closer inspection reveals the strange ritual pits with which this prehistoric sanctuary is girt about. Cairnpapple is a Bronze-Age site. It is unique in its reflection of the changing phases of structure of that era, and the processions of cinerary urns which climbed to its sacred precincts for sepulture ceremonies must have covered many centuries. Why it should have maintained its sanctity in the eyes of successive generations is not hard to understand, for it rises exactly a thousand feet above the sea and commands a prospect that is breath-taking. Beyond the ribbon of the upper Firth the Ochils present a many-coloured wall which, from this ancient burial-place, call to mind pictures of the Valley of the Tombs of the Kings; and beyond the Ochils, westwards, are the far-off, hazy outlines of Ben Ledi and its neighbours. Two thousand years or so later men again briefly took an interest in Cairnpapple. As the sun sinks, the shadow of the hill reaches out towards a place called Silvermine. This, I suppose, must commemorate the seventeenth-century chronicle of one Sandy Maund, a collier, who discovered a heavy chunk of metal containing silver " at the Silver bourne, under the hill called Kern-Popple." When tested, the metal " proved rich, and wonderous rich," and the mine was given the name of God's Blessing. Sibbald, in his *Treatise* (1710) states that a part of the melting-house is still to be seen, but his only other comment on the site is " At the Silver-mines the Poultrie decay, and children are observed to be sickly because of the bad Air."

A mile or so east of Cairnpapple the hill road winds down to the village of Torphichen. Torphichen is snugly sheltered from the east winds by high ground which includes the Tor-phichen Hills themselves, and is the kind of place where one would look for signs of medieval prosperity and sanctuary just as one looks for prehistoric fortifications on the tops of the hills commanding it. Surely enough, among the scattered modern houses rises the tower of the old preceptory, a curious mixture of domestic and ecclesiastical, with sightless Gothic windows under crow-stepped gables of much later date. The old building has suffered many changes, but contains a good deal of interesting detail. For instance, in the north transept, one of the otherwise-plain vault ribs has a black-letter inscription in Latin to the effect that Sir Andrew Meldrum, Knight of St. John, between 1432 and 1439 had safe-conducts to travel to Rhodes, Flanders and England. For this much-rebuilt building is all that remains of the chief seat of the Hospitallers of St. John, first settled here by King Malcolm IV in the twelfth century. The Order was expanded by succeeding kings and absorbed the possessions of the Knights Templars. The Preceptor of Torphichen, or Lord

St. John, held an honoured place in the councils of the nation right down to 1563, when the Lordship was resigned into the hands of the Queen. At one time, all within one mile of the preceptory was sanctuary and hundreds must have fled here to escape the penalties of the law. Some details in the south transept —for example, the filled-in window of lancet type in the east wall—date back very nearly to Malcolm's day, and the archway in the west screen-wall of the crossing is certainly of his time ; but perhaps the most interesting thing in the building is to be found scratched into the plaster at the south end of the west wall of the south transept—a builder's working drawing for one of the vaults, done there maybe two centuries before Brunelleschi made those wooden models of the Duomo still to be seen in Florence.

The Bathgate Hills, the highest point of which is The Knock, rather higher than Cairnpapple, shelter Bathgate from the nor' easters. They also perform the service of concealing it from wanderers on those attractive heights. Bathgate is a prosperous town—of its size the most prosperous in Scotland, I have been told—but it is not a town which it is easy to love at first sight. Nearly a century ago Thomas Gillespie wrote that it had scarcely a house with any pretension to architectural beauty, and the old town he described as " deplorably cramped and filthy." This last is not true any more, but the sum of architectural beauty has not increased in ratio to the prosperity. It is one of those featureless places so numerous in the industrial " waist " of Scotland to which the twentieth century seems to have added no amenities except the usual cinemas and garages and chip-shops, but at least the Edinburgh-Glasgow trunk road has now by-passed it and saved its streets from the added compression of the traffic of Scotland's most soulless highway. The town's earlier prosperity was founded on the weaving industry, and until a century ago the weavers' wives would work at tambouring. The principal article manufactured evidently was something called pullicats. Then came " Paraffin Young," and the jingle of the shuttles passed, to be replaced by new sounds and smells. Coal and iron deposits in the surrounding country were rapidly developed, however, and to-day the iron foundries are the main manufactures both of Bathgate and of its neighbour, Armadale.

The only link with the textile trades of the past is some production of hosiery.

I do not want to imply that Bathgate is either Philistine or traditionless. For example, one retains an impression of massed schools, lofty and imposing, which leaves one a little amazed that the amount of education which seems to be available to the people of the town, and one of the schools at least, the Academy, is widely reputed. It is a classical structure with colonnaded wings, which might be taken for the capital of this community. The endowment came from one John Newlands, a Bathgate carpenter who made a fortune as a planter in Jamaica, but the will seems to have been disputed by the executors in Jamaica, reducing the money available to about one quarter of what it should have been. The Academy dates from 1833. The only building more ancient is the ruin of the parish church, east of the town. It contains a tomb-effigy of a priest in his vestments, worn, mutilated and quite featureless, but still dignified after seven centuries. The figure must have been carved and placed here just a few years before Robert the Bruce presented the lands of Bathgate to Walter Stewart as the dowry of his daughter Marjorie. In those days the curious name of the town was rather different: Bathket or Batket, or even Bathcat. This—if it should be necessary!—seems to go far to dispose of Milne's quaint Gaelic derivation of the name as " windy cow-house ! "

Linlithgow, the county town, lies snugly in a fold at the foot of the northern slopes of the hills over which Cairnpapple and The Knock preside. This fact, indeed, together with the loch beside which the town is built, seem to give rise to the rather curious name itself, for the first syllable certainly seems to signify a stretch of water, and whether the rest means a sheepfold or a little valley does not greatly matter. The town is an odd mixture of thrills and disappointments. It has possessions and traditions far greater than most towns of ten times its size, even in this history-soaked country, yet a tourist in a hurry to get to the Highlands may pass through the entire long length of it with hardly a suspicion that he is missing anything. He enters it suddenly, by way of a grim, grey brewery and a gloomy railway bridge, passes along a mile of street with few apparent amenities, and leaves by a suburb which has simply turned its back on the opportunities offered by a site which is superb. In part, I suspect, the reason why Linlithgow to-day is unworthy of its past is that for generations its numbers have been shrinking. The resources, probably, are just not there. It has its chemical works, it has a celebrated glue-works, but in a nuclear-plastic age perhaps even those products belong with history.

Despite first appearances, the High Street of Linlithgow is full of character. It widens and narrows in the pleasantly unregimented way of medieval towns, and the natural ups and downs of the ground have not been engineered away. Most of the houses are drably Victorian, and will not be much loss when the people who want to broaden and regularise the High Street have their way; but here and there are some good examples of earlier domestic building, not up to the standards of Edinburgh or the Fife villages, but worth preserving all the same. Numbers 40 to 48 are perhaps the best, their crow-stepped gable-ends presented to the street, a stair between the gables holding out promise of interesting interiors which have in fact been destroyed long since. They are of the sixteenth century, and on the south side of the street is another house with the actual date, 1590. The house most closely linked with the country's history is now gone. It is the house where Hamilton of Bothwellhaugh, mentioned in Chapter Five, lay in wait for the Regent Moray and murdered him in revenge for the death of his wife—by the romantic version!—or more probably for political ends. Contemporary accounts have it that the house overhung a narrow part of the street, and that it had a projecting "foreschott" or balcony, no doubt of timber, like most medieval house-fronts in old Scottish streets. The Regent had been well warned, even by Knox, and the dangerous section of the street itself appeared to be known; but Moray was a brave man and counted on spurring smartly past the place where Bothwellhaugh lay in wait. The density of the crowd slowed his progress, and Bothwellhaugh, carefully concealed behind a "washing" on the balcony, had all the time he wanted to take aim and shot his victim through the waist, the sort of wound that offered small chance of recovery in the sixteenth century. The assassin escaped on a horse waiting for him in the garden behind the house, and eventually took ship for France, where Dumas says the boldness of his act won him some admiration.

But in those days when the Palace had its Royal tenants Linlithgow must have been full of interesting houses. There was, for example, the town house of the Knights of St. John ; and about a century ago the removal of lath and plaster in another dwelling exposed the coats-of-arms of fifteen of Scotland's barons and of twenty-two of her earls, suggesting, as one antiquarian writer said, a sort of blue-blooded club. In the sixteenth century the whole of the High Street must have been enclosed by houses with harled or plastered walls of varying tones, embellished by timber foreshots like the one used by Bothwellhaugh for his murderous act. There seems to be no good reason why the street should not be restored to something like its ancient state. The experiment along such lines in the Canongate of Edinburgh has been subjected to a good deal of criticism, but at least it is an attempt to throw off the lazy-mindedness which has allowed most of Scotland's towns to lose their old houses by natural decay. What is needed is some expenditure upon Old Linlithgow to match what must have been spent on the splendidly-appointed new County Council Building at the west end of the High Street.

Whatever may be said about the rest of the town, Linlithgow possesses in the Kirk of St. Michael and the Palace one of the finest groups of medieval buildings in Scotland. Access to these is from the magnificent square near the West Port. The townhouse presides over it : a solid, classical building erected in 1668, approached by a double staircase reminiscent of many a humbler Scots town-house. To the left of the town-house is the lane called the Kirkgate, leading up to the gatehouse, an arched entrance-gateway flanked by barbicans pierced with gunloops and sur-mounted by parapets—a powerful defensive structure of the early sixteenth century, the grim functionalism of it slightly mitigated by sculptured panels carrying the insignia of the orders of the Garter, the Thistle, the Golden Fleece and St. Michael, replicas of older panels.

Just beyond the gatehouse, to the right, soars the Kirk of St. Michael, Linlithgow's parish kirk. Both architecturally and historically, this is one of Scotland's notable churches, and few Scots worthy of the name could emerge from the Kirkgate and come face to face with this lovely medieval monument without some surge of pride—even if Burns did dismiss it in his diary merely with the line : "A pretty good old Gothic church." It is typically Scottish in its massive simplicity and in its very moderate use of ornament, as well as in the treatment of the porch and the corbie-stepped gables of the nave and aisles. The most Scottish of its features, the old crown steeple on the tower, which once made a trio with the steeples of St. Giles' in Edinburgh and King's College Chapel, Aberdeen, was removed early in the nineteenth century because the heritors preferred this to the alternative of restoration. No doubt the buttresses were at one time all topped by statues of saints. The fact that St. Michael himself is the only one of these remaining—in the south-west angle—is probably due to the Reformers rather than the weather, as St. Michael's special position as patron-saint of the town might win him exemption from the attentions of the iconoclasts ; but even he was blown down in 1926 and had to be put back on his pedestal. The church as we see it now is mainly fifteenth-century work and early sixteenth, for the original nave was destroyed in the great fire of 1424. It was, however, one of the foundations of David I, who assigned it to the prior and canons of St. Andrews.

The interior of St. Michael's is even more simple and severe than the exterior, but it is also perhaps even more beautiful. It is Gothic reduced to the bare bones of the style, but the weave and flow of columns and groins is exceptionally fine and inspiring, although it should be kept in mind there was once a timbered ceiling. Probably here too there may have been more ornament prior to the Reformation, although there can have been little time between its completion and the events of 1560. The only surviving pieces are four sculptured sandstone slabs with scenes from the Passion. The best and most complete of them is about three feet long, containing two scenes : the Agony in the Garden, and the Betrayal. Although much worn, all have been sensitively carved, and are to be treasured as among the very few surviving pieces of sculpture from the fifteenth century in Scotland. The west end of the church was once a burial-place for notabilities, but no monuments survive. The vicar of St. Michael's must fairly frequently have had to serve as King's Chaplain, when there was a Royal occupant of the Palace next door. The most celebrated occasion of Royal worship is remembered by the incident of 1513, preceding the disaster of Flodden. James IV was attending vespers in St. Catherine's aisle, the south aisle, his special purpose to implore aid for his adventure into England, when the figure of a man in a blue gown, his long hair hanging down upon his shoulders, pushed through the worshippers, leant towards the King and bluntly foretold ruin if he persisted in his expedition. Waiting for no reply, the visitant passed again among the surrounding courtiers and attendants without a hand laid upon him and vanished in the shadows. The apparition did not dissuade the King, any more than did the ghostly voice shortly after on the Burgh Muir of Edinburgh ; but it made a deep impression on many who saw it, among them Sir David Lyndsay of the Mount, from whom the story passed to George Buchanan and Pitscottie, eventually to be embellished by Sir Walter Scott. Pitscottie, who describes how the visitant " vanished away as he had been a blink of the sun, or a whip of the whirlwind," points to a supernatural explanation ; but there is a local tradition that the distracted Queen had instructed one of her servants to enact the ghost, and that he escaped by a concealed stair, to return across the courtyard to the Palace.

The Palace of Linlithgow is by far the finest lay edifice in Scotland, and has been one of the most impressive Royal residences in all Europe. Mary of Guise declared she had never seen a palace more princely, and she knew the glories of the great French châteaux. Famous as it is, I should doubt if one Scot in a hundred has set foot in it. It could and should be the Mecca of all interested in Scotland's story, for even in its present ruinous state it lives up to its great associations and will awe and delight the most demanding visitor. But why ruinous ? Had this palace been in France or Italy it would long ago have been lovingly restored to the state it was in before Hawley's dragoons burned the roof off it in 1746, and the Lion Chalmer would be glowing with tapestries and the Royal apartments richly furnished again. The building should be shrine and museum in one, and a monument to contemporary Scottish scholarship and craftsmanship.

The site itself is magnificent. Set on a height above a little loch, the Palace has a wide expanse of rolling country to one side of it, the old town to the other. Grassy slopes stretch down from the hill it crowns, and from the north its walls look like some enormous crag flanked by towers and pierced by windows. It is on a square plan, a tower at each corner, and the true entrance, no longer used, is in the east wall and was guarded by a draw-bridge approached by a road which circled St. Michael's Kirk. Over the gateway the Royal Arms, conceived on a generous scale, are carved in the stonework. Entrance is now gained by the south porch. To emerge from the shadows of this south entrance, with its vaulted passage, into the spacious Close or great court-yard is for a moment bewildering. The Close measures nearly ninety feet square, and the enclosing buildings tower so high into the sky that the greater part of the area is in gloom except when a midsummer sun strikes down at a sharp angle. The buildings are not all of one period, but the greater part of the structure belongs to the middle decades of the fifteenth century, although the English Gothic south façade probably dates from about 1500. The sculpture on this and the east façade is known to have been brightly painted in the sixteenth century, and when the now-sightless windows held gay figures and flambeaux glittered in the sparkling waters of the central fountain, the gloom of the courtyard must have given way to grandeur. The four stair-towers in the angles of the walls are slotted with windows corresponding to the spiralling stairs within. One is the King's Turnpike, another probably the Queen's. The central fountain is now greatly damaged, but it is still an arresting piece of orna-ment, with sculptured pinnacles, lions and unicorns, grotesque heads, roses and thistles and medallions. It was erected by James V about 1535. The water for it, incidentally, came from a spring to the south of the town, conveyed first by clay pipes to a stone cistern and then for a considerable way by thick leaden conduits.

On the first floor, the full width of the east side is occupied by the Great Hall, or Lion Chalmer. In its original state, this must have been the handsomest room in Scotland. To-day, roofless and bare, it is still a solemn and inspiring place. Nearly a hundred feet long, with walls 35 feet high, the Lion Chalmer has a magnificent triple fireplace which fills one end, and its west wall has a passage or gallery at clerestory level from which no doubt finely-gowned ladies observed the parliamentary proceed-

The façade of Hopetoun House,
Scotland's finest Renaissance building

The interior of the twelfth-century kirk at Dalmeny

ings which sometimes took place on the floor of the hall in the time of the earlier Stewarts. At the north end of the Lion Chalmer is the Court Kitchen, equipped for the most generous of hospitality. At the other end there is access to a chapel once paved with tiles, some of them with the initials of James IV and his bride, Margaret Tudor, joined by a love-knot. Examples of the tiles may be seen in the National Museum of Antiquities. There are other lordly apartments in the south and west sides; and as Mary Queen of Scots was born in the Palace it may have been in one of them that she first saw light, but if so the birth came about in much grander circumstances than the birth of her own son, James VI, in that tiny apartment high up in Edinburgh Castle. Another room associated with James IV's Queen is the so-called Queen Margaret's Bower, at the top of one of the Tower's. There is, at the other extreme, a dungeon dismal enough to satisfy the most morbid of sensation-seekers, the entrance to it a funnel-like opening, through which the prisoner would be lowered into the chill, dank dark.

A series of castles has occupied this site since early times. David I is said to have tenanted one. Edward I of England built a fort here and spent the Christmas of 1301 in it, and this was garrisoned by the English for twelve years, until a farmer of some such name as Binnoch schemed with the Bruce and hid some armed men in a haycart taking fodder to the alien garrison. But it is not until the Stewarts are on the throne that we begin to hear of the Palace of Linlithgow. James II settled it on his bride, Mary of Gueldres, in 1449; his son settled it on Margaret of Denmark when he married her in 1468; and Margaret Tudor received it in the same way from her husband James IV. As I have said before, Mary of Guise was charmed by it, and probably used it more than did any of the previous queens. It was here, perhaps in the Lion Chalmer, that Lyndsay's great satirical play was performed before the Court. The little Mary Queen of Scots spent her early childhood in the Palace, and indeed caught the smallpox in it; but Linlithgow seems to have been a healthy place, for she caught the disease very lightly, and a hundred years later Parliament met in the Palace to escape the plague which was ravaging the capital. James VI was the last king to give the Palace to his bride as dowry. Nearly all these kings had their parts in adding to the building, and James V is known to have commanded his architect, Sir James Hamilton, the Bastard of Arran, to embellish it. It is ironic that it was the last would-be Stuart monarch, Charles Edward, who, in a way, led up to the destruction of the Palace. In 1745 the wife of the governor entertained the Prince lavishly, even to turning off the water supply and filling the fountain with red wine; but in the following year the redcoats had their revenge and made a bonfire of the place, whether deliberately or no. Yet the governor's wife too had her revenge, for when Hawley refused to intervene to stop his men's incendiarism she stung him by retorting that she could run from fire as fast as he could.

CHAPTER SEVEN

The Upper Frith

IN THE National Museum of Antiquities is a carved stone slab some nine feet long depicting, at one end, a mounted soldier slaying naked enemies and, at the other, a ceremony with priests and animals. Between is a rectangular plaque, framed between axe-heads. On it, clear as the day it was cut, is an inscription in abbreviated Latin which, translated, reads :

IN HONOUR OF THE EMPEROR CAESAR TITUS AELIUS
HADRIANUS ANTONINUS AUGUSTUS PIUS, FATHER OF
HIS COUNTRY, THE SECOND LEGION AUGUSTUS' OWN
EXECUTED (THE WORK) FOR 4652 PACES

The mounted soldier is, of course, a Roman, and his naked enemies are the men of Caledonia. The other scene represents the festival of the suovetaurilia, in which a sow, a sheep and a bull are about to be sacrificed. I find this one of the most fascinating monuments in Scotland. Here is a piece of native Scottish stone, shaped by a citizen of the greatest of ancient empires to be set on the very northernmost limit of that empire, the Wall of Antonine. In its way it is more moving, more impressive than the Forum with its columns of weary tourists going among the temples, or even than the Colosseum itself with a thousand motor-horns echoing from walls that once echoed the shrieks of martyrs, for here the tramp of the legions can be felt suddenly plain on our own familiar ground.

This monument is a " distance-slab." It was set up by the Second (Augustan) Legion to mark the completion of a section of the Wall—perhaps the final section ?—where it met the arm of the sea at Bridgeness. They found it face-downwards, buried in the soil, broken in three pieces, in 1868. The Second Legion, part of Claudius's invasion-force in A.D. 43, moved north to Scotland around A.D. 140 and not only contributed much to the building of the Wall but apparently provided the permanent garrison for some of the forts along the Wall. The Bridgeness slab was found in a spot which, in Roman times, must have projected into the sea as a small headland, and Sir George Macdonald was in no doubt that it marked the extreme eastern limit of the Wall and that, when in position, it would be legible by anyone approaching closely from the sea. The slab is almost the only surviving vestige of this easternmost part of the structure ; but Kinneil House a mile or two farther west is a reminder that at one time this was all part of Kinneil parish, and Kinneil is an adaptation of Cenail, the old Goidelic Celtic word meaning " the end of the Wall," while Grahamsdyke Lane, in the same vicinity, almost certainly marks the line of the ditch which lay in front of the Wall. Thereafter, tracing the direction has involved some of the most delicate archaeological detective work. Sometimes the only evidence has been the displacement of stones in a dyke, or a crack in the wall of a house where made-up ground has slowly settled, or buttresses to shore up a wall which has unwittingly been erected along the edge of the line where the great ditch used to run. Kinneil House itself shows signs of being built on the edge of the ditch. The first real glimpse of the great frontier defence itself, however, is across the River Avon, the county boundary with Stirlingshire.

Most people, looking at a map, are puzzled that the Wall should extend into the Lothians at all. The narrowest distance between the east and west shores of the country would suggest Grangemouth as a better eastern terminal than Bridgeness, saving four miles of heavy construction work and as many as three forts. The Wall, however, keeps to high ground throughout its length. To have struck out across the flat lands to the coast at Grangemouth would have been to throw away a strategic advantage for the little labour saved. Not only this : MacDonald, with a flash of insight which I find convincing, suggested that the Wall, rearing up on the heights, with its forts on the hilltops—an unusual place for the Romans to put them—had a kind of symbolic significance, conspicuous far up into Caledonia as a monument of Roman might. Nowhere would it be more conspicuous than here, at its eastern end. But at the same time it is probably a mistake to think of it entirely as an outermost bastion of the Empire, presenting a front of stern defiance to the naked northern savages as depicted on the Bridgeness slab, for the slab itself, with its passably sculptured figures and its dignified lettering, argues a fairly settled civilisation and a community with resources and some culture. Indeed it is a reminder that the legions were here not for a few years but, with a gap or two, for three centuries. In short, Bridgeness and Bo'ness were within the bounds of the Roman Empire for a span as long as from Cromwell's day to ours, and the wonder is that the remains of those Roman centuries are so few in the area. The three forts, or "stations," were probably at Bridgeness, Kinneil and Inveravon, but all this is largely conjecture or the hearsay of old writers and, the slab itself apart, the only things dug up have been a few coins and potsherds. Yet the Bridgeness slab, like other slabs and altars found along the line of the Wall, appears to have been buried carefully against a return of the legions fated never to take place.

Bridgeness and Bo'ness form one continuous town built on a low shelf along the shore and backed by high ground along which the Wall once climbed. The narrow, constricted site, with its back to the south, have helped to make sad, drab places of those two. Robert Gillespie nearly a hundred years ago writes : "For Bo'ness, with its sewers, squalor and soot, we hold along by the surly shore." The sewers, and perhaps the soot, have probably been eliminated by modern public health requirements ; but the "surly shore" is still a good description, and it would be hard to find anywhere communities blessed with fewer amenities. On one side of the main street are huddles of grey houses crowding about narrow side-streets, and on the other are glimpses of extensive timber-yards and docks, while in the background loom the pitheads to which the place has owed much of its prosperity. For Bo'ness cannot plead poverty as the excuse for its grimness. No doubt it was the very richness of its coal and ironstone deposits which, in the nineteenth century, brought that rush for exploitation which thrust every other consideration aside.

To the casual eye, Bo'ness's most marked feature is the great shore area devoted to timber yards and docks. At the end of the eighteenth century Bo'ness was the third sea-port of Scotland, and its Custom House had jurisdiction over both shores of the Forth from Donibristle and Cramond up to Alloa, while for a time there was a considerable whaling industry equipped with up to eight vessels and two refineries. As a seaport, however, the town has steadily declined, overshadowed by Leith and, since early in the nineteenth century, by its neighbour, Grangemouth. The shore area has gradually spread by reclamation from the sea, and much of this new ground has been utilised for pitheads, for the workings extend far under the Firth, and without reclamation the only area possible for the sinking of the shafts was the narrow strip of the twenty-five-foot beach. This reclamation is a minor epic, in its way, and has a long history. Sir Robert Sibbald, writing in 1710, says that the Dutch offered to reclaim some of the mud-flats of the Upper Frith by means of dykes such as they had built in Holland, and to make them into good agricultural land, with towns and harbours. The offer was not accepted ; but piece by piece the sleeches or slob land—vivid words ! —were dammed to hold back the silt when the tides went out. The potential reclamation area west of Bo'ness is, of course, much greater, as anyone can see who looks down from the Kincardine Road Bridge at the green salt flats to the east ; but Bo'ness has made use of its pit-waste to good purpose, and the ironworks contributed vast quantities of blast-furnace slag in their hey-day of a hundred years ago. From the nineties on, H. M. Cadell of Grange did the thing much more scientifically by forming embankments of the heavy colliery rubbish, within which mud built up to a height of ten feet in ten years. Gales interrupted the experiment by destruction of some part of what had been done, and then waggon-loads of ashes brought by rail, as well as colliery rubbish, were dumped on top of the fertile mud, making solid foundations for timber yards where splendid crops might have been grown.

There is one feature, happily, to look a little incongruous in the drabness of the main street : a pottery. By it hangs quite a long tale. Bo'ness and Bridgeness at one time were nearly as celebrated for their pottery as Prestonpans and Portobello. There is a story that Dutch potters were once settled on this part of the coast, but the native industry proper was established in 1784 by John Roebuck, one of the founders of the great Carron iron-works of Falkirk. He took over a works which had been making coarse wares and began to import fine English clays to make cream-glaze and white stonewares, which were taken by waggon to Edinburgh and there, it seems, sold successfully. Roebuck was elderly, and did not survive long. His work did not stop, however, and a stream of articles came out of the Bo'ness potteries for a century. Punchbowls were among the more successful products, usually with some couthie inscription. In less than fifty years the industry was booming, importing annually no less than 350 tons of clay from Dorset, and the regular Bo'ness complaint of shortage of room was overcome in the usual way, by dumping enough rubbish from the works to extend the foreshore. Everything possible was done to improve the circumstances of the potters by developing various industrial welfare schemes and organising cultural and social activities, while the Bo'ness Potters' Guild grew to be the most promin-ent body of the kind in the town, stealing the trades procession at the old Annual Fair by parading in big beaver hats, tail-coats, white trousers and aprons tied with blue ribbons, bearing tools and emblems of the craft and preceded by brass bands.

The broad stream of history, which flowed so constantly through Linlithgow, seems to have passed by Bo'ness. This is not to say its name is absent from old records. It appears in various forms, the full name, even to-day, being Borrowstoun-ness. Borrowstoun is a modification of burgh-town, and the original village of the name lies a mile inland, between Bo'ness and Irongath Hill, a 500-foot eminence with a superb view anciently known by the inexplicable but much better name of Glour-o'er-'em. There are no really old houses in the town itself, apart from three with seventeenth-century dates which are neither particularly picturesque nor rich in associations. Even those who had a direct interest in the industry and trade of the place clearly preferred to live on the higher ground of the hinter-land.

The principal surviving mansion is Kinneil House, a mile or two to the south-west. It is one of those rather barrack-like big, old houses which are not uncommon in Scotland, built on a generous scale and in spacious grounds with lengthy avenues. The main building is seventeenth century : a rather severe example of that marriage between the vernacular and the Renaissance of which the finest case is, of course, George Heriot's Hospital in Edinburgh. The core of the building is about a century earlier, but its present appearance dates from the time of the third Duke of Hamilton, whose arms, with his wife's, are on the front of the north-east pavilion. Her arms appear on the dexter side, because the Duke, who was an Earl of Selkirk, derived his title through her. The estate seems to have come to the Hamiltons originally by gift of Robert the Bruce, who bestowed them on a Sir Gilbert Hamilton because he slew " the greit Lieutennant of Yngland upon Kinnale Muir." For its most distinguished occupant it had to wait until 1809, when the Duke of Hamilton lent it to Dugald Stewart. In that year the great philosopher had been stunned and incapacitated from lecturing by the death of his second son. He lived for the most part at Kinneil until his own death in 1828. In its seclusion he wrote all his later works, including the *Philosophical Essays*. The tenant most closely linked with the life of Bo'ness, however, was Dr. John Roebuck, the Englishman who contributed so much to the Scottish industrial revolution of the eighteenth century. A medical doctor with a taste for chemistry and metallurgy, he began his industrial career near the other end of the Lothians, at Prestonpans, where he established a sulphuric acid works ; but in 1760 he and some associates founded the famous ironworks at Carron, in Stirlingshire. Ironworks in those times were fuelled mainly by charcoal, as denuded Scots forests testified, but Roebuck set out to make use of the coal which abounded in the waist of Scotland, and in time he leased a colliery at Bo'ness. This proved a disastrous venture. The new seams were soon flooded, and no amount of pumping could clear them. Roebuck, however, came to live in Kinneil House, close to the pit. Hearing of James Watt and his experiments, he brought him to Kinneil, and there the inventor developed his steam engine, an engine which Watt in the end carried through to success. It proved unable to clear the pit of water, but Roebuck believed in it and helped Watt to perfect it in return for a two-thirds share. Unhappily, the Carron Company had sunk thousands of pounds in the equipment for the pit, and this and other ventures brought the doctor so deep in debt that he handed over his share in the Watt engine to Matthew Boulton to cancel a large sum of money which he owed him. His financial interest in the Bo'ness pit likewise vanished. Yet he continued to manage it, and he continued too to live at Kinneil House, where he occupied a good deal of his time with farming. Though worldly success eluded him, few men win such a tribute as that carved on his tombstone in Carriden kirkyard, a tribute not only to his genius but even more to his character and spirit ; but the irony of his career is that his abandoned pit at Kinneil contained a substance, to his eye valueless, but which was in fact the coveted blackband ironstone from which flowed so much of the prosperity both of Bo'ness and of Scotland in the nineteenth century.

The empty harbour of Bo'ness is certainly a depressing sight to-day. Up to half-a-dozen cargo vessels come and go in a week, and where in 1923 there was an export figure of 871,000 tons for coal alone the total figure for 1956 was 11,000 tons. It is small wonder that, at the time of writing, the British Transport Commission is threatening to close the docks, with their annual deficit of nearly £292,000, altogether. The cries of the gulls over the muddy estuary make dismal background music to the decline of this chief port of West Lothian. The mud, indeed, is part of the trouble. Silting has always been a tremendous problem, both here and at Grangemouth. The dredgers are obsolete, and the mud has to be dumped well below the Forth Bridge, which makes a long haul and an expensive one. The dredging costs at Bo'ness in an average year are as high as £12,000. But the picture is by no means hopeless. Modern suction dredgers, for one thing, would speed up the task of channel clearance, and the mud that is at present lost could be dumped on the land reclamation sites. It has even been suggested that fixed suction gear might be installed to transfer the silt from the harbour straight on to the flats to the west of the town. Another big problem to be solved is the poor railway communications. Due either to rail transport or to the silting, ships have had to lie off Grangemouth, waiting to unload, instead of making use of Bo'ness, their obvious alternative. Given resolute action to solve those two problems, however, there is no reason why Bo'ness should not enter on a new phase of usefulness. Partly this is due to the fact that the town itself has plenty of work. The colliery is expanding and eventually will employ 1500 miners. The iron foundries are still prosperous, and there are other industries. But more important than local work is the great background expansion of industry in the midland " waist " of Scotland, between Forth and Clyde, the expansion on which so much of the increasing prosperity of Grangemouth is based. Grangemouth need not destroy her ancient neighbour, indeed will not. She cannot cope with the traffic, and as mid-Scotland goes on developing she will be less and less able to cope with it except by expanding facilities for larger and larger vessels, which means that she must stretch her harbourage seawards, down the Firth, towards Bo'ness. There seems every likelihood that the two towns will become a single economic unit, and a unit of swiftly increasing importance, especially if, as one writer has suggested, Britain becomes integrated in a free-trade scheme with Western Europe, which could revive the old Baltic traffic which once filled the Forth estuary with shipping and created such lasting links between Scotland and Scandinavia. It may or may not mean that Bo'ness will to some extent lose her identity ; but on the other hand it would inject a new stream of vigour into that coastal strip of West Lothian which for some generations now has gradually resigned itself to live on its past.

The coast road east of Bo'ness and Bridgeness winds up by Carriden into gentler farming country. It skirts the low hills that protect Linlithgow and its loch from the north, and comes into the wide, shallow carse between the county town and the coast and there meets a side road which winds away firthwards again to Linlithgow's ancient port, Blackness. I doubt if there is any place in Scotland where it is less easy to conjure up past bustle and prosperity. In the fifteenth century it was the highest sea-faring port on the south shore of the Firth, and in 1481 an English fleet thought it worth while to burn the shipping in it. In Georgian and perhaps even early Victorian days it seems to have been something of a bathing-resort. To-day it is a huddle of houses which look only too well aware of the awful sense of anti-climax which they rouse in anyone coming eagerly down the twisting lane into the village. The muddy beach offers no temptations, and a derelict pier adds to the weight of depression. The only pleasing prospect is the distant view across the Firth to Culross, or down it to the Bridge. Even the one great focus of interest in the village, the Castle, is difficult to recognise in the stolid building out on the point, crowded about with the dull buildings of an ordnance depot and aproned with an ugly modern jetty. Blackness is yet one more example of our national inability to make the best of a site endowed by nature and by history. Public money could be much less well-spent than in subsidising a few of the good people of Kirkcudbright to flit to Blackness, there to gut and refurbish and decorate the village and turn it into the pretty spot it could be, with a curving causeway leading round the bay to a Castle stripped of all its modern encumbrances.

Blackness, like some other Scottish castles, is perhaps more impressive inside than out. Built right out on the point of the Black Ness, the fortifications take the shape of the snout of land and on plan look like a ship making out into the Firth with a central tower representing the main-mast. This central tower is the oldest surviving part of the Castle, and the walls of it at least date from the fifteenth century. At that time the sea appears to have come close to the walls on two sides, a moat completing the triangular stronghold. In the sixteenth century the French twice occupied the Castle in attempts to sway the political tide in their favour : first, in 1548, when Henri II sent M. d'Esse to persuade the Scots into agreeing to a marriage between Mary and the Dauphin, and secondly under the regency of Mary of Guise. The Sheriff of Linlithgow drove out the French garrison in 1560. A dozen years after there came to it from France the Queen's dowry of 50,000 double ducats, later handed over to the Regent Morton. Under James VI Blackness became an instrument of coercion in the King's hands in his war against the Kirk, a sort of Bastille which loomed for recusants. In 1584, when Andrew Melville denounced the late queen as Nebuchadnezzar, he escaped the Blackness dungeon only just in time ; and three years later the ministers who refused to pray for the executed Mary in the precise terms required by James did not escape that dungeon. John Knox's son-in-law himself saw the inside of the Castle when he refused to condemn the Assembly. The final recognition of Blackness's importance as a key-point is in the Act of Union, when it is mentioned as one of the four fortresses to be maintained in full military strength; and the authorities who, in 1870, turned it into a gun-store and powder-magazine may have thought they were merely fulfilling the historic obligation laid upon them!

Two roads lead out of Blackness. The one to the left turns eastward, skirting two low hills called the Binns. On their slope and facing the afternoon sun is a spreading, castellated mansion, the House of the Binns. The castellations are an early nineteenth-century modification, but the house itself belongs to the early seventeenth century, when the " lands of the Bynnis " were purchased by Thomas Dalyell, Deputy Master of the Rolls to James VI. Dalyell enlarged an older structure and embellished it, notably with some superb plaster ceilings evidently completed in the time of Charles I. The plasterwork includes rich friezes of exotic fruits, and even portraits of Dalyell and his celebrated son, together with a very good example of the Scottish Royal Arms of the period, which is thoroughly Scots, even if the rest of the plasterwork shows strong Italian influence. The most notable thing about the House of the Binns, however, is the personality of the great Tam Dalyell. General Tam was the son of the man who bought and rebuilt the house. His visage, with portentous beard, looms from more than one portrait, and his spirit clings to the relics of him which are shown: the Scots Bible, the riding-boots and spurs, the chair and sealskin-covered trunk, the sword and dagger, above all perhaps the vast comb which once combed the beard which he swore not to cut until Charles I's son was restored to his throne. Tam Dalyell is that hounder of the Covenanters whom we have already seen on the field of Rullion Green, but that common picture of him is all too incomplete, for he was one of the most dynamic personalities which the three Lothians have produced. His name, oddly enough, first appears on the pages of history as a signatory to the Petition of 1637 against the forced use of the Book of Common Prayer in Scotland; but when it came to a choice between the Crown and the Covenant, Tam Dalyell's loyalty was for the Crown. He was a soldier, and from the start he fought on the King's side in the Civil War. Again from the start, he transferred his loyalty to Charles II. Captured at Worcester, he lay for some months in the Tower before making his escape to the Continent. There for a time he shared exile with Charles, but he was too forceful a man to be content with the inactivity and intrigue of the exiled Court and he went into the service of the Czar of Russia, whose armies he did much to reorganise. He fought with the Russians and was ennobled by the Czar, Alexis Michaelovitch. In 1666 Charles recalled him to Scotland, and it was then that the "Bluidie Muscovite," as the Scots called him, earned his repute as an enemy of the Covenant; but it is not so well known that the executions following Rullion Green so offended his sense of justice that he resigned from his position as head of the Scots forces. From this time dates his interest in his estate of the Binns, which he did much to plant and cultivate. Later, he returned to his command of the forces, and in 1681 he raised three companies of dragoons, a regiment quickly known as the Royal Scots Greys,—not, as usually thought, because of the dapple-grey horses, but because the uniform was of a grey cloth which General Tam Dalyell received a special licence to import. He died before he could receive the baronetcy that Charles II intended for him, but it came to his son from James VII and II. Many legends have grown around his memory. Perhaps the most impressive is the tale of his playing cards with the Devil, and winning, when the Devil in his fury picked up the card-table and threw it at him. It missed and fell in the pond where the Scots Greys first watered their horses, and the sequel is that in the dry summer of 1878 a marble table was duly discovered in the pond, a table which is naturally now among the treasures of the House of the Binns.

Between the Binns and Queensferry is one of the most out-of-the-world corners in the county. With the shale-oil industry only a few miles to the south and the Rosyth dockyards within sight to the north, it is astonishing how much these few square miles contain of what is ancient and hallowed. The Midhope Burn winds through the midst of it, among fields and pastures and woodland which seem to belong with the past as completely as the hoariest of ruins. As one turns north from the main road to make for Abercorn, there are two big, old houses close by: first Philpstoun House, a fine, simple example of a Scots laird's house of the seventeenth century, with white, harled walls and crow-stepped gables, and then Midhope Castle of a century earlier, rather grim and embattled-looking. Then the road swerves away from the burn again and, quite suddenly, one is in Abercorn. This is the very heart and core of these few unspoilt acres. The old forest trees that shelter the village seem to conspire to fence it off from the urgent present, and in the watching quietude one feels conspicuous. The few houses of the village are not so old, except perhaps for the big, rambling manse, which appears to have seventeenth-century features, but there is a sense of rich old mould about the place which brings with it an awareness of decay and mortality. In the lovely old churchyard the awareness of mortality is intensified, not merely by the crouching tombstones with their inordinately high proportion of death's heads, but by the silver-green patina everywhere. Even the church itself has the squatness of an old man who has sunk in upon himself and bowed his head a little under the weight of years. It is disconcerting, at first, on closer approach, to find that everything seems to belong to the post-Reformation period, that there are even seventeenth-century dates carved on details of the church ; but presently one notices the built-up Norman doorway in the shadow of the Binns aisle, a simple chevroned arch enclosing a tympanum with lozenge pattern, a ghost-like relic of the older church. In the vestry is preserved something of still greater antiquity, a fine carved cross-shaft of whitish sandstone which, if not such an important monument as the great cross in the kirk at Ruthwell, in Dumfriesshire, at least belongs to the same epoch and must be something like twelve hundred years old. With it are other fragments. They point to a very ancient sanctified site here at Abercorn, and indeed the place is mentioned by Bede. The seventeenth-century church itself, however, is peculiarly interesting for the insight which it gives into social history. The Binns aisle, mentioned above, is a somewhat cave-like annexe in the shadow of the pulpit in the dim light of which Tam Dalyell must have been able to dose through the sermon if he chose. The first Thomas Dalyell is buried in the aisle. So is his wife, Janet Bruce, and her epitaph contains the following rather unusual lines :

The Upper Frith

Within the closure of this narrove grave
Lye al those graces a good wife could have
Bot on this marble they shall not be read
For then the living envye wold the dead.

Unlike the Binns aisle, the Hopetoun family loft dominates the church. It is probably the finest example of a laird's loft in Scotland and was designed by no less an architect than Sir William Bruce. The vault is below the gallery, which is decorated with repetitions of the family arms and with fruit and flower motifs, and there are retiring-rooms panelled in Memel pine, one of them having a " squint " through which the family might observe that the minister was back in the pulpit and so bring their refreshment to an end.

A mile or two away is another and much greater project of Bruce's, Hopetoun House itself. It stands in the midst of one of the most notable pieces of landscape gardening in Scotland, and is now the seat of the Marquess of Linlithgow. Great Renaissance houses, judged on an English or Continental scale, are few in the north, and enthusiasts have compared Hopetoun with Versailles. One may at least agree it is the greatest of all Scottish mansions of its kind. The claim that it is the greatest example of the Scots Renaissance style is more difficult to accept, for there is little or nothing Scottish in the style although the house is the work of Scottish architects from first to last. Indeed, it is the antithesis of the Scots method of treatment, which expresses the interior arrangements of a house in its exterior. Hopetoun is designed in the first place for its exterior effect, and that is quite superb whether from the east or from the west.

In spite of its classical balance and regularity, Hopetoun was not built all in one piece, but was added to from time to time over a long period. Bruce began it during the minority of the first Earl of Hopetoun, but his part in it came to an end in 1703. This original structure may best be seen in the central block as viewed from the west. There is a great deal of English feeling in it. The building was substantially completed by Bruce's pupil, William Adam, whose contribution has been depreciated by some modern writers perhaps a little unfairly. The completion of Hopetoun was a challenge to any architect, and Adam proved he could achieve work on the grand scale, so far as we know to the satisfaction of his cultured and no doubt exacting patron. The great colonnades to north and south were carried out in the twenties and thirties of the eighteenth century. It is quite true there is a certain lack of unity in the immense façade, and there may have been some borrowing from Vanbrugh and even Wren ; but all the same the architects were men of vision and considerable originality. Adam died in 1748. His more famous sons completed the interior decoration. They were faithful to their father's concepts and a whole epoch lies between the richly dignified elegance of the Red and Yellow drawing-rooms at Hopetoun and the dainty, *fin-de-siècle* decorations at Culzean, or Mellerstain. Robert Adam was on terms of friendship with the Hopetoun family, and the second Earl's brother was with him in Italy for some part of the time of the epoch-making stay which contributed so much to the " Adam style." On the staircase there is some handsome wood-carving which, with reservations, has been compared with the work of Grinling Gibbons. The furniture is interesting too, and some of it may have been made in Italy to the designs of Robert Adam. This is noteworthy, because it is not often in great Scottish mansions that the furniture or furnishings can be claimed as being closely associated with the building itself. Another feature unhappily unusual in Scotland : the collection of paintings is worthy of the house. The cream of the collection was brought together in Italy in the earlier years of the nineteenth century, and includes a Rubens, three Van Dycks, and pictures by Canaletto, Cuyp and a number of lesser masters. The prospect from the house on a summer evening must be one of the most gracious in the country, with shadows of beech, oak and chestnut lengthening over the grassy avenues and lawns which stretch towards the Firth and its blue waters spanned by the gilded red cantilevers of the bridge.

In these last seaward parishes of this account of the Lothians there is an embarrassment of riches where historic mansions are concerned. I say an embarrassment because I feel that too much of any single sort of fare is hard to stomach. The fact remains that Abercorn and Dalmeny, with their green parks and woodlands and magnificent shore sites, cried out to be made into pleasances for the retreat and recreation of men of power or favour, so that keeps and mansions neighbour one another nearly all the way from Blackness or Cramond, or their ruins haunt the fields. I shall pick out only two more, and one of them must be Dundas Castle. It lies about half-way between Kirkliston and South Queensferry, and the old structure has had a new house built on to it rather more than a century ago. The old part belongs to the fifteenth century topped by battlements of about a hundred years later. The Dundas family, descended from one Huttred in the time of David I, is by far the oldest in the parish. The fountain in the grounds vies with the sundial at Lennoxlove as one of the most interesting pieces of garden ornament in Scotland. It combines a sundial with its other function. An inscription records that Sir Walter Dundas erected it in 1623, and proclaims in a most baffling Latin that guests are welcome, but warns off the evilly-disposed.

The only town on this rather choice part of the coast is the Royal Burgh of South Queensferry. It nestles largely between the old sea cliff and the sea. Like other towns along this piece of coast it is oddly lacking in the amenities which mark the towns and villages along the opposite shore of the Firth, but in certain lights at least there is still a good deal of charm about its winding main street, although the esplanade to the east is a mere parking-lot and a queuing stance for the Forth ferry. The prosperity of Queensferry to-day is largely bound up with the huge red brick distillery which dominates it. It still profits from the shore trips of the naval men whose units constantly lie out in the anchorage, but the great concentrations of heavy ships which used to lie both above and below the Bridge belong to other times. Even I can remember the narrow waters grey with Beatty's battle-cruiser squadron and its attendant screen, but now a lone air-craft-carrier and a destroyer or two do no more than point to the emptiness of the estuary where the greatest fleet-surrender of all time took place in 1918. To look up the Firth from the Hawes Pier on a winter afternoon, with the wan, red glory of the sun doubled in the long, oily swell is to re-live the sweet melancholy of one's first look at Turner's *Fighting Téméraire*. Here, perhaps more than in any other of Britain's former great bases, and at such a time of year and day, one murmurs " Ichabod ". . . And yet Queensferry should be a gay place. It has scenic advantages which many a resort on the Swiss or the Italian lakes cannot match; but the Scots have a curiously heavy touch when it comes to making the most of their scenery, or perhaps it is the climate that takes the hearts out of them. There are some good features in the town around which some discerning patron or provost of the town might build better things. The seventeenth-century parish kirk has its points. The tolbooth is good, in the east-coast manner, with its Dutch bell gifted to the town by "the seamen of Queensferrie" in 1694. There is Plewlands House, too, a three-hundred-year-old mansion saved from destruction for road-widening only by public outcry, and now handed over to the National Trust for Scotland on the understanding that the interior be converted to modern flats. And at the extreme east end of the town is the celebrated Hawes Inn, in part dating from the seventeenth century. The inn faces the jetty from which ferry-boats have plied across the Firth to North Queensferry for well over a hundred years. It must have been a colourful place when the coaches went over, as late as the time of the second *Statistical Account*: the "North Mail," the "Defiance" to Aberdeen, the "Coburg" to Perth, the "Antiquary" to Dunfermline and Perth. According to the *Account* the fare for a four-wheeler was 7s. 6d., actually rather more and relatively much more than the largest car costs to-day. Both Scott and Stevenson knew the inn and introduced it into their romances.

The dominating feature of Queensferry, however, is the Forth Bridge. I mean, of course, the Forth Railway Bridge, not the Road Bridge now a-building, but it is to be feared that between the two great viaducts Queensferry will shrink to a mere scatter of rooftops noticed in the passing. It is not, perhaps, the function of a book on the Lothians to do more than to mention either bridge; but on the other hand both their economic and social and also their spectacular effects on the Lothian scene make them in a sense part of the Lothians, just as they are a part of Fife. I am confident that of the two bridges the old one will remain the greater wonder. Considered in relation to its time, it must be accepted as one of the great material achievements of man on earth, like the Pyramid of Cheops or the Wall of China, although its existence is likely to be short compared with theirs.

Its impact on the eye is more immense than the impact of any of the seven wonders of the ancient world can have been. From as far off as the Pentland Hills it looms up, end on, against the base of the Ochils like the three pyramids at Ghizeh together. From the Hawes Inn, it darkens the sky with its might and majesty. From Hopetoun or Dalmeny, it has the beauty of a spider's web spun in the angle of two twigs.

The greatness of the old bridge surely lies in the fact that in the year of its completion, 1889, heavy engineering was still in the phase of high adventure. The new bridge is not an adventure. The basic problems have long ago been solved and it is just another job. But the old bridge was a supreme challenge, a challenge made critical by the collapse of the first Tay Bridge in 1879, and I do not think I am romancing when I say that the spirit with which the challenge was taken up is subtly materialised in the bridge itself—in the utter functionalism of the three huge cantilever-spans, like a warrior stripped of all his trappings for the life-and-death test, and this, be it remembered, in an era when the naked truth was almost invariably veiled in ornament. The epic quality of the task should be evident to anybody looking up at the bridge from the Hawes Pier. If not, then I recommend the mammoth paper which appeared in *Engineering* for 28th February, 1890, the week when the Bridge was opened by the Prince of Wales, a paper suitably embellished with drawings and reproductions of the enterprise from start to completion, with fascinating views of the great cantilevers growing out towards one another like gigantic oak-trees. The basic difficulty in bridging the Firth at this, its narrowest point, is the depth of the two main channels, which is around 200 feet. As early as 1818 an enterprising Edinburgh engineer planned a suspension bridge, using the island of Inchgarvie for one of the piers, and it is Inchgarvie which supports the central cantilever of the present Bridge. The piers were formed by floating huge caissons to the positions required, sinking them there, and pumping in compressed air so that men could work on the foundations on the sea-bed as though they were on dry land. Materials were passed down to them through air-locks. Seventy years ago though it is, they were not dependent on pick and shovel, for both concrete-mixers and hydraulic spades were in use. The caissons were slowly filled with concrete and the granite piers built upon them. The girders of the approach viaducts, at either end of the Bridge, were actually raised to their full height of 130 feet above high water by carrying them up with the piers as they were built. But the truly Homeric part of the achievement is the construction of the three cantilever spans. As I have said, they grew like trees. The steel tubes which form the main members of the cantilevers are 12 feet in diameter, or in cross-section comparable to a London underground " tube," and these were the " branches " which crept outwards into space, 50, 100 and at last 150 feet above the sea, added to yard by yard by the workmen who manned the hydraulically-operated cradles which moved forward with the work. It is not surprising to learn that 57 workmen died in the construction of the Bridge. The perils of submarine building and aerial engineering were added to by such untoward things as a smallpox epidemic to cope with which the hulk which served as a cement store-ship had to be converted to a floating hospital ! Indeed the labour problem was itself a minor epic. The project attracted thousands of workers, skilled and casual, from half the countries of Europe, and colonies of lodgings grew up to accommodate them, colonies which contemporary accounts make to sound rather like Klondyke towns, complete with drinking-dens. Then again, the weather was a vital factor : in storm or blizzard or fog there had to be a halt to this great challenge to nature's forces, and special trains had to be called up to return men to their homes who came from greater distances—Leith, perhaps, or Dunfermline. At last, after seven years, on 14th November, 1889, the final link-up of the spans was completed. It was a delicate operation requiring certain temperatures to expand the girders and so bring the appropriate rivet-holes opposite to one another, but nothing could better illustrate the skill and precision which went into the building of the Bridge.

The great new road bridge brings to an end an era. For nine hundred years this point where headlands of Lothian and Fife reach out to one another has been known as the Queen's Ferry, because it was across this channel that the consort of Malcolm Canmore was ferried to and fro on her journeys between Edinburgh and her husband's capital of Dunfermline. The name of her brother, Edgar the Atheling, is commemorated in the name of nearby Port Edgar. If queens and kings and dynasties have changed, the ferry has remained. Until now, it has meant a sea-voyage to cross from Lothian into the Kingdom of Fife, or since 1890 the almost equally romantic aerial rail journey among the majestically-wheeling, red cantilevers of the Bridge ; but soon it will be possible for the ordinary man or woman to walk from the one county to the other, and sooner or later the last of the ferry-boats will rust away, and the Ferry will become as much a figment of legend as the Queen who was linked with it. Perhaps they will call the new bridge the Queen's Bridge, bestowing on it a name with a double significance.

Below the Bridge, the shore makes a great bend to the north-west, ending in Hound Point, and the entire headland is richly wooded. This is Dalmeny Park, the estate of the Earl of Rose-bery, stretching for three or four miles south-eastwards to the point where the Almond enters the Firth. Though hemmed in by the city and by the heavy traffic of the Great North Road, making to and from the Bridge, this must be one of the loveliest properties in the south of Scotland. Copses and woods of mag-nificent old timber shelter parks and pastures, and here and there a cultivated field, and all is rolling ground, with sudden glimpses of distant hills or of the flashing waters of the Firth. The highest mass within the policies is known as Mons Hill, famed for its carpet of snowdrops at the end of winter. An interesting feature at the Cramond end of the Park is the Hunter's Craig. Otherwise called the Eagle Rock, it is a mass of stone near the shore, and on the east face of it has been carved some sort of a figure. It is largely obliterated, but past generations have seen in it the form of an eagle and have attributed it to the Romans. The Ancient Monuments Survey does not rule out the possibility of its being Roman work, because the Roman station at nearby Cramond was a very important one ; and since Roman naval craft regularly used the haven at the Almond's mouth it seems not unlikely that a landmark such as this rock would attract the men who carved the altars and monuments left by the Roman occupation. Dalmeny House is not itself older than the first half of the nineteenth cen-tury, although the estate has been in the possession of the Rose-bery family since the seventeenth. The oldest habitable, though not inhabited, structure on the estate is Barnbougle Castle, superbly situated on a little promontory of the coast, once the seat of the Mowbrays and later of the Earls of Haddington, but it was almost wholly restored by Archibald Primrose, fifth Earl of Rosebery, the great Liberal Prime Minister. Here he may have written some of those percipient and eloquent speeches which can still stir us to-day as they stirred his hearers in the seventies and eighties. Here certainly is stored much of the material on which that learning was based which won him election to the rectorship of all four Scottish universities, and under its roof there is still a rich store of historic relics.

The village of Dalmeny lies a matter of half a mile from the Park, as attractive a hamlet of its sort as there is almost anywhere in the Lothians, although it consists of a straggle of cottages. It is, however, merely the simple, modest setting for one of Scotland's two or three finest architectural gems, the parish kirk. Dalmeny Kirk dates from about 1160. Not just an arch or a doorway of it dates from this time, but the greater part of the church, which is therefore the most complete Norman relic in Scotland. It is tiny, but choice—under one hundred feet long. In plan, it could scarcely be simpler : a nave, a chancel, and the apse which serves as sanctuary. The original western tower fell as early as 1480. This, as Professor Hannah remarked, was a weakness of Norman towers, as the Normans rubble-filled the walls of their churches as they never would have done with castles which had to withstand the battering-ram. The tower was restored before the Second World War by the efforts of the minister himself. The most beautiful feature of the exterior is the south doorway. Surmounted by a short length of intersecting arcade very similar to the arcade of Leuchars church across in Fife, the door itself is narrow and set in a recess flanked with nook-shafts, and the arch above is richly sculptured—very richly for a Scottish church—with creatures grotesque or legendary, zodiacal signs, monsters from the bestiaries, and so on. The interior of the church has no doubt been modified considerably, but it is still an exquisite study in Norman building. The chancel arch, the moulded ribs of the quadripartite vault, the sculptured corbels sing out in the otherwise unadorned simplicity like a passage of perfect engraving on a piece of Queen Anne silverware, and the light falling into the little, raised sanctuary completes the impression of something exceptionally choice. Here in this tiny place of worship, perhaps more than anywhere else, one is moved by the thought of how long the Lothians have been tenanted by pious and sometimes scholarly and cultured men. The ancient coffin before the south door calls to mind the fragments of the cross-shaft at Abercorn, the Roman altars and hypocausts at Musselburgh, the hidden hoard of silver on Traprain, the relics of forgotten rites on Cairnpapple hill, and one comes sharply to realise how the Lothians have been the cradle of so much of Scotland's history.

Index

INDEX

Abercorn, 173-6, 183
Aberlady Bay, 73, 79
Adam, Robert, architect, 20, 74, 113, 176
Adam, William (father of Robert), 20, 175-6
Addiewell, 142
Agriculture *see* Farming, Market-gardening
Allermuir, 115
Almond Water, 143-6, 149-150, 181
Amisfield, 54, 74
Antonine Wall, The, 163-5
Armadale, 142, 154
Arniston, 99, 114
Athelstaneford, 47-9, 55
Auchendinny House, 113
Avon, River, 164

Baberton House, 129
Balerno, 124-6
Balfour, Arthur James, 14, 61
Balfour, Rev. Lewis, 131
Barnbougle Castle, 181-2
Barondale, 103
Bass Rock, 30, 44, 54, 63, 65-8
Bathgate, 142, 152, 154-5
Bathgate Hills, 137, 152, 154
Bavelaw, 125, 126
Belhaven, Lord, 17, 20
Belhaven Bay, 37
Biel, 17, 20
Bilston Glen Colliery, 99-100, 101, 104
Binns, The, 172-3
Binny Craig, 152

Black Agnes, Countess of Dunbar, 39, 40, 43
Black Law, 123, 125
Blackburn, 142, 143
Blackhope Scar, 24, 25
Blackness, 170-2, 177
Blair, Rev. Robert, 48-9
Bleak Law, 16
Bo'ness, 165-170
Bonnyrigg, 105
Borrowstoun, 167
Borthwick Castle, 26-9, 44, 103
Bothwell, fourth Earl of (James Hepburn), 15, 27, 44-5, 46-7, 51, 71, 88
Bothwell, fifth Earl of (Francis Stewart), 28
Bothwellhaugh, Hamilton of, 121, 156-7
Bow Castle, 23-4
Bridgeness, 163-6
Broxburn, 141, 151
Broxmouth Park, 45
Bruce, Robert the, 111, 120-1, 149, 155, 161, 168
Bruce, Sir William, 113, 175
Burdiehouse, 91
Burnet, Dr. Gilbert, Bishop of Salisbury, 31-2

Caerketton, 115, 132, 133
Cairnpapple, 13, 152-3, 154, 155, 183
Cairns Castle, 116, 124
Cakemuir Castle, 27
Calder House, 144
Camp Hill, 93, 94

187

Index

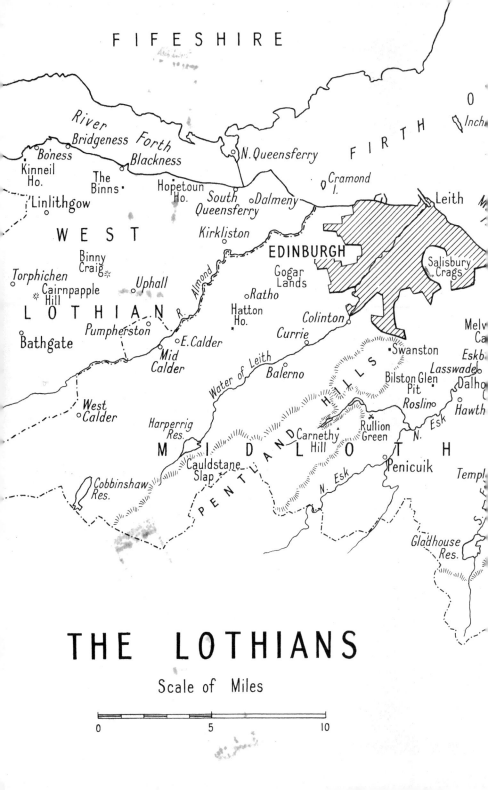

THE LOTHIANS

Scale of Miles